Scapegoated Capitalism

Ben Irvine

Oldspeak Publishing.

First published in 2016.

All content © Ben Irvine 2016.

All references and links to sources are available from
www.benirvine.co.uk

With special thanks to Rebecca Watts for her assistance.

Scapegoat: *Any material object, animal, bird or person on whom the bad luck, diseases, misfortunes and sins of an individual or group are symbolically placed, and which is then turned loose, driven off with stones, cast into a river or the sea, etc, in the belief that it takes away with it all the evils placed upon it.*

– Funk and Wagnall's Standard Dictionary of
Folklore, Mythology and Legend

Contents

1

Exploding the truth

People are always quick to call evil what they do not know. The unknown sprouts fear. It spreads like an infection, burrowing into every facet of their lives. They need a scapegoat, someone to blame. Fingers are pointed, accusations are made, and a target lands on somebody's back. They grow angry. They turn violent.

— Kelseyleigh Reber

When, in 2010, environmental lobby group 10:10 unveiled its short promotional film *No Pressure*, viewers generally reacted with shock, dismay and incomprehension – a collective "what the...?" which was about as far as you can get from the mass enlightenment hoped for by the filmmakers. Written by Richard Curtis and featuring a cast of celebrities and volunteers, the film comprises a series of vignettes in which people who are reluctant to take personal action on 'climate change' are gruesomely blown to pieces.

The first victims are two schoolchildren. They are killed following their failure to raise their hands when a teacher asks her pupils who among them is willing to 'cut their carbon emissions'. 'No pressure... it's your choice', she tells the young dissenters sympathetically, before pressing a detonator on her desk. The rest of the children, screaming, are splattered with flesh and gore, while the teacher calmly wipes blood from her own cheek.

Next up, a business leader asks for a similar show of hands among a group of employees; again, there is 'no pressure'. 'Great, that's nearly everybody!' he crows, then reassures a handful of naysayers – 'it's no problem, your choice' – before pressing a detonator and exploding them, prompting more screams and flying body parts.

The camera then cuts to retired footballer David Ginola who is visiting the training ground of his old team Tottenham Hotspur, where, as part of a PR exercise, various players and staff members are reciting the club's green credentials. Unimpressed, Ginola shrugs his shoulders Gallically, receives some now-familiar assurances – 'that's just fine... no pressure' – and is graphically blown up.

Finally, actress Gillian Anderson reads a voiceover as the credits begin to roll. 'Care to join us? No pressure', she concludes snidely. We then see her sitting, headphones on, in a sound booth, and she is asked by her producer what *she* is going to do for the great cause; apparently, her contribution so far is insufficient. 'Are you kidding me?' she replies, and... well, you can guess what happens. The film's refrain is projected sinisterly onto the bloodied window of the booth: 'cut your carbon by 10 per cent – no pressure'.

What the....?!

By way of an explanation, the director of 10:10, Lizzie Gillet, described the film as an attempt to bring the 'increasingly threatening' issue of climate change 'back into the headlines while making people laugh'. Obviously, the film achieved only one of those aims with any success, as well as making the issue of climate change seem 'increasingly threatening' in not quite the way intended. Following a media outcry – as well as criticism from numerous environmental groups – *No Pressure* was withdrawn after a single day in circulation. 10:10's website stated that 'many people' found the film 'extremely funny', 'but unfortunately some didn't'. The Guardian, which was a key collaborator with the 10:10 movement and had exclusive rights to *No Pressure*'s premiere, insisted that while the film may have been 'somewhat tasteless', it was 'an imaginative attempt to challenge public apathy over climate change', adding – 'and, highly unusually for attempts to communicate about this subject, funny too', although the addition was later redacted.

Of course, retaliatory humour isn't always beyond the pale. You might argue that 'climate change deniers' are legitimate targets for brutal satire (or even satirical brutality). Perhaps the film is no different in spirit to the much-loved scene in the British sitcom *Fawlty Towers* where John Cleese pokes fun at Nazis.

Whatever you think about the comedic value of watching children publically executed, the film's sadism would be harder to defend if the charges levelled against climate change deniers are unreasonable. Or, indeed, if the charges are worse than unreasonable. Environmentalism, beneath the nuances of its various guises, is characterised by a tendency to assume that whenever people harm nature, or nature harms people, we should pursue moral recriminations within society. Although this tendency can be noble, it is also on a spectrum with the nastiest and most enduring form of human sadism. As human beings, we all have a talent for making ourselves feel better by blaming other people for our sins and misfortunes, especially when we are in the majority. The real explanation, I believe, for the bizarre film *No Pressure* is that the gratification enjoyed by its advocates, and others like them, amounts to a still-prevalent form of bullying that's rarely talked about today: scapegoating.

Scapegoating! It's the untold story of our modern lives, and the story of this book. Once you've seen scapegoating for what it is, you see it everywhere – not just in environmentalism but in education, health, the media, housing, welfare and politics. This book takes a tour of the history and psychology of scapegoating, and then explores its modern incarnations, with all their devastating effects.

We've all heard about the problems of modern society, and we've all been told who is to blame – those nasty businesspersons, bankers, individualists and capitalists who are ransacking not only the environment but the values and institutions we hold dear. Right? Capitalists are destroying social responsibility and replacing it with selfishness, competitiveness and greed. Right? We need a revolution, governance for all. Right?

Like I said, once you've seen what scapegoating really is, you see it everywhere. Even in yourself.

2

The history of scapegoating

Hell is other people.

– Jean-Paul Sartre

There are many forms of scapegoating. The simplest and most familiar can be seen in the attempt by individuals to evade responsibility or censure through attributing blame not to themselves but to other individuals, animals, objects or events. Children do it prolifically – "I didn't break the vase, mummy; it was so-and-so's fault', or "the dog did it", or, "the wind blew it over". And so do adults – even more so, although we kid ourselves that we have grown out of that sort of thing. We can spot the tendency less readily in ourselves than in other people – in the spouses who blame each other for their own infidelity, in the boss who arrives home and kicks the cat after a stressful day at the office, in the shoddy workman who blames his tools, or in the dissolute who blames the drink.

Though devious, scapegoating makes intuitive sense when it occurs between individuals; there are obvious potential advantages to be gained through seeking exoneration or recompense. Even blaming animals and natural forces can provide exoneration for an individual. Less intuitive – indeed, downright disconcerting – is the long and ubiquitous history of individuals and minorities being scapegoated by *groups* of human beings. Charlie Campbell's fascinating book *Scapegoat: A History of Blaming Other People* abounds with examples.

In some of the strangest cases, the victims of these persecutions were animals, as attested to by the word 'scapegoat', which was coined by William Tyndale in his 1530 English translation of the Bible. The book of Leviticus describes a 'Day of Atonement' on which, over 1000 years before the birth of Christ, two goats were sacrificed to God on behalf of 'the people'. After the first goat was slain and set alight, the second was driven alive into the wilderness. William Holman Hunt's painting 'The Scapegoat' depicts this doomed creature, abandoned in a bleak, rocky landscape.

Goats are not the only animals to have been victims of scapegoating. We could just as accurately talk of scapesheep, scapepigs, scapeoxen, scapefish, scapeturkeys, and many more. In 1840 on the remote island of St Kilda, 110 miles off the west coast of Scotland, a violent storm killed scores of fishermen after their boats capsized. When the seafarers' bodies began to wash up on the shore, they were accompanied by a dishevelled-looking beast, barely alive, with a heavy black beak. It was a Great Auk, a large flightless North Atlantic bird. The surviving islanders promptly declared it a witch, blamed it for causing the storm, and stoned it to death, in one of the last known sightings of this now extinct species.

A common theme in scapegoating by groups is the power of nature, and of paranoia. Scapegoats are often targeted after natural disasters, or at times when natural forces are particularly consequential, such as immediately before harvests or at times of seasonal change (when there is a greater threat of disease). The scapegoaters assume that natural calamities follow from sin, either in the sense that sinners deliberately and malevolently cause misfortune, or in the sense that misfortune is a punishment for sin.

These spurious inferences – which could be described philosophically as 'morality category errors' – most likely have evolutionary roots. The ancestors of the human race lived in close-knit bands of hunter gatherers to whom outsiders typically posed a mortal threat. As a result, our sensory systems evolved to be hypersensitive to the presence of hostile human agency; a false positive in this domain was far less costly, in survival terms, than a false negative. Upon the slightest provocation – the snapping of a twig, the rushing of the wind – we tend to jump to conclusions about being stalked, flanked or watched by shadowy conspirators. We discern intelligent agency where in reality there is none, and we explain the discrepancy by conjuring up supernatural beings such as spirits, ghosts, zombies, demons and witches. We detect espionage in animals or inanimate objects, and we even construe the whole of nature as capable of judging and punishing us. At this extreme, religion emerges; the very force that menaces us becomes our saviour, as though we were suffering from a cosmological Stockholm syndrome.

The evolved human propensity to associate misfortune with sin gives rise to an urge to neutralise wrongdoing so as to prevent future misfortune. Culprits must be identified and dealt with, and, since the accusations are so insubstantial, any culprit will do. Animals, especially domesticated ones, are easy targets and cannot defend themselves against allegations. But nor can vulnerable human beings – and, by virtue of being human, they make more plausible sinners. In September 1666, the Great Fire of London raged for four days and destroyed eighty per cent of the old city. Londoners were eager for a culprit, so the police arrested a crippled and mentally defective Frenchman by the name of Robert Hubert. Under extreme torture, he confessed to starting a fire in Westminster. However, the authorities soon realised that the conflagration didn't reach Westminster, so Hubert promptly changed his confession, claiming to have thrown a grenade into the open window of a bakery on Pudding Lane. After he was executed by hanging, it transpired that Hubert wasn't even in England at the time of the fire.

Not everyone agreed with the verdict. The London Gazette wrote that the fire was 'the heavy hand of God upon us for our sins'. Later, even the official account admitted that the fire was an act of God. Yet the widespread assumption among Londoners that their collective guilt had been divinely punished did not lead to collective atonement; the punishment of only one sinner, Hubert, was deemed sufficient to atone for the sins of the majority.

This scapegoating double-standard can be found repeatedly throughout antiquity.

In Athens, outcasts were rounded up and imprisoned. During the agricultural festival known as Thargelia, two were selected as scapegoats. They were led around the city amid much praying; the idea was that they would absorb the sins of the men and women, respectively. After being genital-whipped, the unfortunate pair must have thought things could hardly get any worse; they were then stoned and burned to death outside the city walls.

In Albania, slaves were imprisoned in the Temple of the Moon. Each year, a slave who showed signs of being especially insane was selected to be a scapegoat. He was held in chains on public display for a year before being anointed with oils and stabbed to death. It was believed that his corpse would take on the sins of the people.

In Tibet, a man was declared to be the 'King of Years'. With his face painted half white, half black, he was forced to sit in the marketplace, where passers-by were invited to discharge their sins onto him. He was then chased into a cave outside the city. If he survived there for a year, he was brought back and the whole process was repeated.

In Rome, as part of the New Year celebrations, a man was dressed in skins to represent the year past. He was led through the streets then beaten with rods and driven out of the city, all in the hope of prompting a good harvest. Later in the year, during the Saturnalia festival, the Romans were permitted to indulge in all manner of sins, from feasting and drinking to dancing and copulating, after which one person was punished to relieve the guilt of all.

The bullying of an individual to assuage the anxieties felt by a majority is not a trait confined to the human race. In times of overpopulation or food scarcity, hens often peck to death low-ranking members of the flock; that's where the term 'pecking order' comes from. Other species act similarly. For instance, in wolf packs the lowest-ranking animal – the 'omega' wolf – is often mobbed and attacked by the other wolves. Usually the omega rejoins the pack afterwards, but he tends to be ostracised repeatedly. He is especially vulnerable to attack whenever status displays among mid-ranking wolves get out of hand; the wolves dispel the tension by turning their ire onto the omega. In the end, he may give up and leave the pack permanently, but curiously when this happens the remaining wolves respond by howling plaintively; the loss of the omega compromises their coherence as a group, so they soon find a new scapegoat.

The omega wolf isn't always physically the weakest member of the pack. But that's not so curious when you think about it. The omega serves a social function, so the stronger he is, the better equipped he is to endure that role. Perhaps, indeed, the stronger he is, the more likely he is to return to the pack after being bullied, as though optimistic that he can one day climb the hierarchy. As far as the other wolves are concerned, the 'ideal' omega wolf is strong enough to bear the brunt of being scapegoated but vulnerable enough to be picked on, vulnerable in the sense of lacking sufficient aggression and allies to ward off the attacks.

Many of the scapegoats chosen by human groups similarly display strength as well as vulnerability (surviving for a year in a cave, for instance, is no mean feat). Indeed, the scapegoats we cherish the most – the ones we mythologise – tend to display the greatest strength. The stronger the scapegoat, the better equipped he is to bear the burden of our collected sins. Jesus Christ is obviously the most famous example of a burden-carrying scapegoat, and there are many other martyrs in the history of Christianity who demonstrated similar forbearance. Other religions have comparable figures. In China, worshippers rub the stomach of a fat, smiling Buddha so as to pass their suffering on to him; his expression remains joyful throughout, an indication of his strength. In Aztec mythology, Tlalzelotl was a goddess of purification; she was able to forgive people by eating their sins.

There are also plenty of mundane examples of the strength of the scapegoat – including the fact that human beings, not just immortals, were thought to be capable of sin-eating. In the Middle Ages, funerals were often attended by a specialist who was paid to take on the sins of the deceased. The 'sin-eater' would sit next to the corpse and consume food and drink that was passed over it, thus symbolically consuming the dead person's sins and ensuring him or her a smoother passage to heaven. The role was widespread until surprisingly recently; in Britain the last known sin-eater was a Shropshire farmer called Richard Munslow, who died in 1906. Though technically a scapegoat, he was far from being the wretched and weak figure usually associated with the condition.

The strength of the scapegoat is further indicated by the connection between leaders and scapegoating. Before democracy took hold, monarchs, emperors and other rulers were accredited with immense influence. They were believed to be intermediaries between the divine and the earthly, and so, when disaster struck, they were held accountable by the public. Rather than accepting blame or admitting fallibility, canny rulers sought to channel popular anger onto one or more scapegoats; after all, even God, the supreme ruler, had a scapegoat, namely, the Devil (horned and hoofed no less).

Obviously, any form of malevolence that can thwart a ruler must be formidable. Sometimes scapegoats were selected from within the ruling echelons. When a crisis hit, a culprit was sought out who had enough responsibility to be held accountable but who was remote enough from the centre of power to divert blame safely away from the ruler. These ministerial lightning rods proved so useful that rulers would go to great lengths to retain them, or to bring them back quietly once the furore had subsided. The downfall of the ruler was often expedited by the loss his favoured scapegoat. During the reign of England's King James I, one of his closest advisors, George Villiers, took the blame for numerous debacles. Eventually Villiers was assassinated, prompting another courtier, Thomas Wentworth, to remark: 'it is said at court there is none now to impute our faults onto.'

The importance of a loyal scapegoat was often imprinted early upon rulers. In childhood, many monarchs were granted 'whipping boys'. It was considered unseemly that a future ruler should be whipped for his misbehaviour, so he was provided, in effect, with a personal scapegoat who would take the punishment instead. The idea was that the heir would form a friendly bond with his scapegoat, and therefore be reluctant to misbehave. Far from being unenviable, whipping boys were often selected from the upper reaches of society and were educated alongside their master. Many were ennobled later in life.

As well as keeping their scapegoats close, rulers sought to create, or invoke, powerful culprits whose malevolent influence was widespread and diffuse. The goal was to divert attention away from the leader's failings while simultaneously drawing attention to his protective qualities. As H. L. Mencken famously put it, the 'whole aim of practical politics is to keep the populace alarmed (and hence clamorous to be led to safety) by menacing it with an endless series of hobgoblins, all of them imaginary'. History is replete with such hobgoblins, these powerful insiders who were also believed to be dangerous outsiders. Freemasons, the Illuminati, Catholics, Satanists, Communists, David Icke's Giant Lizards, and, perhaps above all, Jews have been accused of mounting conspiracies against the public. In Russia in 1903, a publication entitled *The Protocols of the Elders of Zion* warned of a Jewish plan for global domination. Supposedly, the Jews were trying to distort the press, subvert the morals of gentiles, and control the economy. Influential figures from Henry Ford to Adolf Hitler took these allegations seriously, and many people today still do. Paradoxically, the reputation of Jews has never been helped by their links to money, power and cultural sophistication. It is notable that many other persecuted communities, such as the Stedinger in Germany and the Templars in France, had their wealth confiscated before they were exterminated.

But, undoubtedly, the longest-standing so-called conspirators, with their covenants, midnight gatherings, spells and subtle marks of identification, were the many women (and some men) who were accused of being witches. Although they were scapegoats, witches were perceived to be terrifyingly powerful; after all, any person who can raise a tempest, destroy a harvest, cause diseases and infertility, and fly on a broomstick, is hardly a pushover. Widely believed to exist in Europe and America from around the fourth century to the eighteenth, witches continued to be invoked sporadically in the centuries beyond (and today at least half the population of Africa still believes witches exist). In a Papal Bull in 1584, Pope Innocent declared that witches were the 'Enemy of the People'. Such pronouncements were typically followed by mass waves of witch-hunting, usually precipitated within each community by a local accident, death or grudge. (Or, worse, as Keith Thomas documents in *Religion and the Decline of Magic*, in many cases the so-called 'witch' was an old woman who had been refused alms by her accuser; assailed by pangs of conscience, the accuser would claim to have been 'cursed' by the accused.)

Eighty per cent of 'witches' were women. As Campbell remarks, 'the only great powers that women were credited with at this time were supernatural ones'. Ironically, sometimes the accused women were targeted *because* they possessed worldly talent; their worldly talent was misogynistically deemed to be supernatural. In Alexandria in the fourth century, a woman called Hypatia was accused of being a witch. She was a philosopher, mathematician, musician, head teacher, and civic leader, and her prowess sparked political jealousy. A mob, led by a minor Christian cleric, kidnapped Hypatia and dragged her through the streets to a church. There she was stripped, skinned alive with oyster shells, dismembered and burned to death.

The charge of witchcraft was effective precisely because it was so easy to bring and so difficult to gainsay, in both cases because relevant evidence wasn't available; you can neither prove nor disprove an accusation, for instance, of raising a tempest. Not that the accusers didn't try to 'prove' their claims. Suspects were tortured horribly, their feet and legs crushed and genitals burned, to extort confessions. The forehead and feet of the accused would be checked for signs of horns and hooves, the torso for signs of a third nipple; the flimsiest indications would suffice. Witches were thought to be able to make themselves beautiful or ugly at will, which hardly left much scope for exoneration. Most infamously, witches were trialled by 'swimming'. A suspect was tied up and dropped into a deep stream or pond. If she drowned, she was innocent; if she floated she was a witch ('the water shall refuse to receive them in her bosom, that have shaken off them the sacred water of baptism', as King James I explained). You can hardly get more unfair than that, although in 1573 a recluse named Gilles Garnier was convicted of being a witch on the basis that a wolf which had attacked a local child had 'looked like him'.

Whether through simple-mindedness or exasperation, some of the accused witches acquiesced in the charges. As marginal figures, chronically under suspicion, they may have felt that magical power was a compensation for their loneliness. Some may simply have been at the end of their tether: 'I made up my confession ... choosing rather to die than to live', said one long-suffering witch during her trial.

But eventually the rest of the population, too, became exasperated by witch-hunting. The trials were orgies of recrimination, which tore communities apart. Often the initial accusations stemmed from petty resentments which, inevitably, were grotesquely exacerbated by the ensuing investigations. Famously, in Salem in the US, a series of witch trials took place between February 1692 and May 1693, leading to the execution of twenty people. Communities began to realise that the trials were far worse than the alleged crimes. People also began, correctly, to discern spite or fraud in the accusers; when Lady Alice Kyteler was charged with 'sorcery' in Ireland in 1324, many of her accusers were also her debtors (she managed to flee to England, but that didn't prevent her servant from being flogged and burned at the stake: even scapegoats have scapegoats). The banquets and celebrations accompanying the execution of witches began to seem more callous and sinister than the suspects themselves.

Communities likewise became mistrustful of 'witchfinders', the officials who orchestrated the trials and the carrying out of the court's judgments. Self-styled 'Witchfinder General' Matthew Hopkins, whose career flourished in seventeenth-century England, was paid twenty shillings per conviction – a month's wages for a labourer or footsoldier. The payroll for a witch trial also included an executioner, a judge and his assistants, and a carpenter (to build the gallows or other instruments of death and torture). The suspicion grew that these beneficiaries were doing little more than bleeding the public dry.

Around the same time, a similar bottom-feeding frenzy was taking place throughout Europe, in a slightly different context. Religious clerics sometimes conducted bizarre court trials of insects and other pests accused of menacing a community or its crops. These proceedings were basically esoteric debates about whether the pests' behaviour was natural as God intended, malice on the part of the creatures (perhaps involving the machinations of evil spirits), or a punishment from God. Attempts were made to excommunicate the pests, via legal pronouncements or religious incantations. If the latter were unsuccessful, often the reason given was that the congregation had failed to pay their tithes promptly. The trials dragged on and on, typically until nature itself intervened, for which the clerics claimed credit. There were also, of course, monetary rewards for all those involved in conducting the cases.

Campbell recounts a poignant moment from his researches. In the archival records of a sixteenth-century court action against (believe it or not) some weevils, there is a passage explaining how, at one stage during the eight-month-long proceedings, the judge attempted to compromise with the weevils by offering them a tract of land in which they could live without further impeachment. Campbell continues the story:

> The weevils blithely continued their existence, unaware of these goings-on. And so the prosecution and defence found themselves in court again. The latter stood up and claimed that the specified land was not suitable for his clients, not being fertile enough for their needs. The prosecution shrieked that it was admirably suited for them, having plenty of trees and shrubs of various kinds. The court decided that an expert should examine the site and submit a written report of its suitability as a refuge for the insects. For this the expert was paid 3 florins, while 16 went towards clerical work. The vicar received 3. I would love to relate how this nonsense all ended but history has dealt with it in a much more appropriate way, the final page of the court records having been destroyed by insects of some kind – perhaps even the defendants themselves.

As well as further demonstrating the corruption involved in spurious legal cases such as these, Campbell's anecdote symbolises perhaps the deepest of the failings that arise from the moralisation of misfortune: *ignorance of how nature really works*. When misfortune is spuriously linked with sin – whether sinners are deemed to be directly and malevolently responsible for a natural calamity, whether they are deemed to be indirectly responsible through incurring God's retribution, or whether, in both cases, sinners are deemed to be capable of preventing future misfortune through atoning for their sins or others' – the result is a deepening of ignorance among the accusers, despite their best efforts at engaging with the situation. When collective efforts amount to worse than nothing, there are lamentable psychological forces at work.

3

The psychology of scapegoating (then)

Men, it has been well said, think in herds; it will be seen that they go mad in herds, while they only recover their senses slowly, and one by one.

– Charles Mackay

Although the history of scapegoating by groups is shocking, it is easy to appreciate how in some situations the practice could have seemed effective. Desperate times, which prompt desperate measures, tend, through sheer probability, to be followed by an improving situation, that is, a transition from extreme to less exceptional conditions. This transition, which statisticians call the 'regression to the mean', may have given scapegoaters the false impression that their cruelty had been effective, thus encouraging them to do the same again next time, followed by another regression to the mean, and so on.

We might also wonder whether some past examples of scapegoating by groups were based on an inchoate awareness of issues that today we recognise to be legitimate, an awareness that further explains why persecution seemed like a sensible strategy. For instance, although the scapegoaters were ignorant of the causes of disasters, it is true that individuals and communities can always to some extent prepare for disaster, and this preparedness (or a lack of it) may sometimes legitimately be the subject of moralisation. Similarly, although diseases have external origins, the susceptibility of human beings to illness depends to some extent on physical factors which can be controlled. Many scapegoating rituals were conducted in the name of 'purity'; destroying the scapegoat was believed to wash away the sins of the people. This horrid notion at least has a tenuous link to reality: diseases can indeed be brought on by poor hygiene, and arguably poor hygiene sometimes deserves moral scrutiny.

There is little doubt, however, that one of the primary motivations for scapegoating by groups was that the practice made the perpetrators *feel better*, for reasons ranging from the malign to the mystical. Seeing another person suffer can elicit sadism, *Schadenfreude*, or simply a relieved sense that 'there but for the grace of God go I'. Similarly, the moralisation of misfortune may have provided a kind of metaphysical comfort to the scapegoaters; presumably they found it less frightening to believe that natural disasters occurred for a malevolent reason than for no reason at all. In turn, scapegoating no doubt helped survivors to achieve a sense of closure after a traumatic event, or to experience reassurance in the face of impending adversity; an activity as demonstrative as scapegoating may have discouraged anxious rumination and encouraged faith in the authorities. Above all, scapegoating by groups bonded its perpetrators together. Unity feels intoxicatingly good, especially when times are bad.

Yet, of course, the overall effect of scapegoating by groups cannot, by any stretch of the imagination, be considered positive. A semblance of legitimacy is just that, a semblance: the perpetrators neither recognised nor understood the real causes of the problems for which scapegoating was spuriously deemed to be the solution. Even the power of group unity is superficial when it is not deployed in tackling the genuine sources of past or potential problems. When brought about through scapegoating, the merits of unity are swamped by the demerits of ignorance and cruelty – cruelty, moreover, which threatens all the group members, since each of them might soon have their turn as victim.

Indeed, this ever-present threat provided another powerful motive – perhaps the most powerful motive of all – for scapegoating by groups: the avoidance of being scapegoated. It was a case of *find a scapegoat or be scapegoated*. This dynamic was further compounded by the fact that groups of scapegoaters, through their ignorance, continued to be maximally vulnerable to disasters, thus making scapegoating continually seem like a suitable response. During the plague that ravaged Europe in the Middle Ages, among the many scapegoats upon whom the disease was blamed – including Jews, witches, and assorted misfits – were *cats*. Nothing more clearly illustrates how scapegoating is accompanied by chronic ignorance of the real causes of a disaster (the cats would have eaten the rats that carried the bacterium-infected fleas).

When all members of a group end up worse off as a result of each of them trying to achieve a positive outcome for himself, they are engaged in what is technically called a 'tragedy of the commons'. The phrase was first used by Garrett Hardin, who was alluding to the fact that a shared pasture (a 'commons') may be depleted by individual farmers who seek more than their fair share of usage of the land; the collective 'tragedy' of a depleted pasture more than cancels out the advantages sought by the individual farmers. But the phrase can also refer to any situation where individuals seek advantages over each other but suffer outweighing disadvantages as a group. Scapegoating fits this description.

We can imagine each member of a scapegoating group initially pointing the finger gleefully at the unfortunate victim, each seeking to avoid the hard work of contributing to a genuinely cooperative and realistic effort to improve the situation, each seeking to avoid being scapegoated himself, and each therefore contributing instead to a collectively harmful and futile spiral of persecution in which the persecutors become trapped just as much as the persecuted. In any tragedy of the commons, the participants become trapped because as soon as the tragedy has been set in motion it becomes difficult for each participant to reverse his initial involvement; upon such a reversal the consequences for him as an individual would become even worse; he would suffer the same negative consequences as the rest of the group but without the personal gain. Worse still, in the case of scapegoating, anyone who deliberately forwent the advantages of scapegoating might himself soon, by insinuation, be at risk of persecution. This was frequently demonstrated in local witch-hunts; anyone refusing to denounce the accused typically came under suspicion themselves, whether because of a perceived affiliation to the accused or a perceived rebellion against the authority of the accusing group.

A tragedy (of the commons) occurs when members

of a group fail to take personal responsibility for avoiding the tragedy; far from being some sort of impersonal visitation upon the group, the tragedy consists in the failure of individuals to behave responsibly. The lack of responsibility shown by scapegoaters can be detected in the execution methods that were common to the practice. By stoning victims to death, or driving them off cliffs, the members of scapegoating groups sought to avoid individual culpability for the killing.

Yet this eschewal of responsibility simultaneously points to a subtler, deeper feature of the psychology of scapegoating, a feature that, paradoxically, belies each individual scapegoater's failure to accept responsibility. Consider the cases of scapegoating by groups in which the perpetrators believed that their own sins were being atoned for by the victim. Such a belief implies that the scapegoaters implicitly recognised that their victim didn't deserve the punishment. After all, the very act of attributing blame to someone else so as to avoid one's own personal atonement implies an acknowledgement, on some level, of personal culpability; perhaps this acknowledgement was part of the reason why each scapegoater desired not to be the individual who murdered the victim.

Insofar as a scapegoater displays a belief in his own culpability *and* a belief in his vindication, he displays a textbook case of 'self-deception'. A self-deceived person consciously believes something that he subconsciously knows is false. The explanation for this inner contradiction is that his conscious belief is a strategic reaction to his knowledge; he knows something inconvenient or shameful, so this knowledge is overwritten by his conscious mind.

Psychologists point out that each of us has a 'self-serving bias' – an inclination to believe that we are a good person – and one way in which we manifest this bias is by deceiving ourselves about our flaws. In turn, self-deception also enables us to lie more convincingly to others. Hence, the scapegoater who blames someone else for his own flaws exonerates himself precisely because he knows he is to blame. He passes the buck precisely because he knows the buck is his to pass. He deceives himself about his guilt so as to feel better about himself, and – as a member of a scapegoating group – so as to join in more convincingly with others in accusing a scapegoat.

Tragedies of the commons and self-deception can also be detected in cases where scapegoats were held to be responsible for causing a natural disaster, such as when witches were accused of raising tempests. In blaming the victim, the individual accusers sought all the usual benefits of scapegoating, while the group as a whole was compromised in all the ways described above. Concurrently, such cases involved self-deception insofar as the victims were deprived of a genuine opportunity to prove their innocence, for instance when witches were trialled by swimming, or convicted on the basis of entirely normal bodily markings. The accusers must, on a subconscious level, have been aware that they were giving the accused no chance; in other words, the accusers were aware that the outcome they were trying to secure was not justice but the beneficial effects of scapegoating. The accusers deceived themselves about the validity of their approach precisely because they knew of its deviousness; in other words, they lied to themselves insofar as they understood on some level exactly what they were doing.

Ultimately, these scapegoaters also lied to themselves about their guilt. Initially they did not seek to project their guilt onto the scapegoat – at no point did they believe, consciously or otherwise, that they were guilty of the crime of which they unjustly accused the scapegoat – but, through forcing the scapegoat to atone for that crime, they simultaneously forced him to atone for their subconscious guilt about treating him unjustly.

Indeed, in all cases of scapegoating, the scapegoat ultimately atones for the guilt that his accusers feel subconsciously about scapegoating him. Looking at the examples I have discussed so far, this perverse outcome may have occurred even among group members who didn't initially want to blame the scapegoat for anything at all. The pressure to conform caused by the logic of a tragedy of the commons may have been enough to trigger the involvement of many reluctant scapegoaters. Anyone who initially believed that the group was in the wrong – that the whole farrago of scapegoating was pointless and harmful – would have perceived how much personal risk this belief entailed, and for that reason may have gone along with the others. Some people, of course, may simply have lied to the others without lying to themselves. However, in such a situation self-deception would have been a safer, and likelier, course: there is no better way of making a lie plausible than believing it. Saddest of all, even the group members who went along with the accusers without lying to themselves – those who were consciously aware of their guilt – may have derived some satisfaction, even if only a sense of relief, from the scapegoat's demise. The maliciousness of scape-goating sweeps through groups like wildfire.

4

The psychology of scapegoating (now)

*So you think that money is the root of all evil? Have
you ever asked what is the root of all money?*
– Francisco d'Anconia, in Ayn Rand's *Atlas Shrugged*

Like human nature, scapegoating didn't get left behind
in the distant past. Just ask Yoko Ono, who was
accused of breaking up the Beatles. Ask Gaëtan
Dugas, aka Patient Zero, who was blamed for the
spread of Aids in the US. Ask David Beckham, whose
effigy was burned after his sending-off saw the
England football team crash out of the 1998 world cup
– and, for that matter, ask any football manager who is
fired when the players don't pull their weight, or when
the board signs useless players. Ask Peter Mandelson,
the New Labour minister who was sacked three times
and twice returned to office under Tony 'Teflon'
Blair's UK government. Ask your parents: 'they fuck
you up', insisted poet Philip Larkin. Ask Prince Philip,
accused by Mohamed Al-Fayed of killing his son,
Dodi Fayed, who died alongside Princess Diana in a
car crash in Paris in 1997. Ask any cyclist who is
shouted at by a frustrated car driver. Ask the
Birmingham Six and the Guildford Four, all of whom
spent decades in prison after being falsely convicted of
acts of IRA terrorism. Ask the innocent souls among

the captives still languishing in Guantanamo Bay. Ask Barry George, the misfit loner who was acquitted six years after being found guilty of the murder of TV presenter Jill Dando, a case which remains unsolved. Or ask any other poor innocent who is luridly tried in the press.

And yet – media witch-hunts are not real witch-hunts. And miscarriages of justice are exceptions which prove that, on the whole, in the modern world justice predominates and injustice isn't entirely irreversible. Gone are the days of barbarous, murderous scapegoating, wherein the victims had scant chance of a fair trial and zero chance of a retrial. As Steven Pinker recounts in his masterpiece *The Better Angels of Our Nature*, most forms of violence and persecution have been declining in the West over the course of millennia. Humanity's nasty side has foundered on such benevolent forces as the imposition of law and order, the kindling of individual human rights during the Enlightenment, the spread of mutual gains by means of commerce, the escalation of technological development, the rise in prosperity and living standards, the increasing rapidity and ease with which information can be transmitted over large distances, the continuing spread of democracy, the decline of militarism and xenophobia, the popular embrace of cosmopolitanism, and, above all, the victory of reason and science over ignorance and superstition.

By insulating us against the worst that nature can throw at us, and by disincentivising us against throwing the worst we can at each other, the apparatus of modern life has drastically reduced the threat of the brutal kind of scapegoating seen in previous centuries.

But, of course, one of the reasons scapegoating is still with us is that sometimes scapegoaters actively want their scapegoat to stick around. Just as wolves want their omega wolf to remain with the pack, there are all sorts of groups today – from peer groups and work teams to families and sports teams – that keep a scapegoat close, for various reasons.

For instance, there may be unresolved tensions among members of a group, and whenever those tensions come to the surface, the scapegoat is the perfect outlet. Just as wolves turn their ire onto the omega whenever the pack members' jostling for position threatens to spiral out of control, bickering human beings collectively turn their ire onto a scapegoat in order to clear the air. This diversionary strategy, like all forms of scapegoating by groups, is a tragedy of the commons. By attacking the scapegoat, each group member seeks refuge from an escalating conflict, but, as a result, all the group members suffer an outweighing disadvantage, insofar as the underlying issues that provoked the conflict are not resolved to anyone's satisfaction. Chronic mutual enmity is the price to pay for unity based on scapegoating.

Simultaneously, group members in such a situation also display self-deception, insofar as they allow themselves to believe that through scapegoating they have genuinely resolved their mutual differences. Deep down, they know that their enmity is undimmed, and, indeed, they know it has been intensified by its latest airing. That's precisely why they deny their enmity to themselves, telling themselves instead that they and the other group members are the best of friends, united in their opposition to the scapegoat. The very basis of their conscious unity is their ongoing subconscious enmity, a smouldering enmity that will sooner or later burst into flames again.

Members of a scapegoating group may also want their scapegoat to stick around if they have problems not just with each other but as individuals. The scapegoat affords each group member the opportunity to gain relief from his personal problems by attacking the scapegoat: the scapegoat is the proverbial cat that gets kicked, although, in real terms, the attacks suffered by the scapegoat may be verbal or physical. Sometimes the scapegoat may be blamed for directly causing a scapegoater's problems. For instance, someone who is exhausted after a long day's work may say to a scapegoat: "you tire me out." Other times, a person may simply take out their frustration on a scapegoat. For example, in sweltering weather someone who is hot and bothered may start being pettily critical towards a scapegoat: "you're breathing too loudly", "why are you looking at me like that?", "you're irritating me." Whether taking out his problems on the scapegoat or blaming the scapegoat for those problems, the scapegoater deceives himself into believing that he is behaving constructively; he knows his problems are getting on top of him, which is precisely why he kids himself that he is dealing with them through scapegoating.

Of course, none of this would count as scape-goating by a *group* if not for an added ingredient: the group members support each other's attacks on the scapegoat. This added ingredient ensures that the scapegoat is defenceless against each attack. Whereas he might have been strong enough to defend himself against a single bully, he is subdued by a group of bullies. Scapegoaters who support each other in this way are, again, involved in a tragedy of the commons. Not only do they secure support for their own future mistreatment of the scapegoat, but they receive a further advantage: the advantage of not having to bother helping the other scapegoaters solve their problems. After all, it is much easier to chip in when a person is attacking a scapegoat than to help that person genuinely deal with his problems. But, as a result, such scapegoaters suffer an outweighing disadvantage; they condemn each other to facing their problems alone. Meanwhile, the scapegoaters deceive themselves into thinking that they are part of a united group. Their unity, which is centred on their mistreatment of the scapegoat, is in fact a self-deceptive strategic reaction to their mutual indifference. Each group member knows that the others don't genuinely care about his problems; hence, each group member deceives himself into believing that they do care.

In turn, when members of a group perennially abandon each other to their problems, a tense atmosphere is more likely to arise within that group – and the scapegoat bears the brunt. Conversely, a tense atmosphere discourages group members from helping each other with their problems – and the scapegoat bears the brunt. These two forms of scapegoating – one an aggression pact within a group, the other a means of dispelling group tensions – are in fact two sides of the same coin, the warp and weft of a scapegoating group.

In the above examples, the scapegoater's problems are largely external to him. Life's various problems range from being completely external in origin to completely self-inflicted. Most of us spend most our time dealing with external problems; self-inflicted problems, by their nature, are more easily dealt with. Scapegoaters, however, typically have both kinds of problems. People who routinely deal with their problems through scapegoating, and thereby neglect their problems, accumulate self-inflicted problems as well as external problems. Common self-inflicted problems include drug abuse, alcoholism, reckless gambling, unsuitable sexual liaisons, overeating, irresponsible spending, or generally choosing a lifestyle that is incompatible with being happy. In lashing out at a scapegoat, a person with self-inflicted problems may sometimes blame the scapegoat for causing those problems. For instance, someone who eats too much may say to a scapegoat: "you *make* me eat, by stressing me out." Alternatively, the scape-goater may simply take out his self-inflicted problems on a scapegoat; an alcoholic, for example, might beat up a scapegoat when drunk.

Whether taking out his self-inflicted problems on a scapegoat, or blaming the scapegoat for causing those problems, the scapegoater lies to himself about his self-destructiveness; deep down, he knows he is to blame for his problems, which is precisely why he lashes out at the scapegoat instead of looking inwards. Once again, this would not count as scapegoating by a *group* if not for the fact that group members support each other when they take out their self-inflicted problems on a scapegoat. In backing each other up in this way, they again seek the advantage of securing future support for their own attacks on the scapegoat, as well as the advantage of not having to engage with each other's problems. However, as a result, the scapegoaters suffer the outweighing disadvantage of their ongoing self-destructiveness and their ongoing indifference towards each other's self-destructiveness. And simultaneously they deceive themselves into thinking that they are unified as a group. Deep down, they are well aware of their indifference towards each other, which is precisely why they consciously deceive themselves into thinking they are unified.

Sometimes it only takes one scapegoater to blight a whole group, if that person is an authority within the group. When an authority figure chooses scapegoating rather than facing up to his problems (self-inflicted or otherwise) the other group members may join in out of misplaced loyalty or fear. In turn, they may mimic the authority figure's scapegoating strategy when 'dealing with' their own problems. In this way, scapegoating becomes entrenched within the group.

What sort of person is selected to be a permanent scapegoat by a group? It is easy to see how the weakest group member could end up being scape-goated. Being the weakest, he is likely to be the most frequent target of attacks, thereby gradually slipping into the role of scapegoat.

Sometimes, however, a stronger candidate inadvertently puts himself forward for the role. In a group whose members are inclined towards inflicting problems on themselves, any member who attempts to alert the others to their self-destructive behaviour is likely to face a struggle. After all, when someone with self-inflicted problems is confronted with the truth about those problems, he typically responds self-deceptively. Rather than face up to the shame of his culpability, and the shame of the impact of his problems on others, he vehemently denies the truth. He diligently employs every rhetorical technique of evasion – slippery reasoning, righteous indignation, shifting the blame, abusive words or actions, changing the subject, and so on – and he does so, moreover, with increasing vigour the more reasonably and carefully his culpability is pointed out to him. In the Shakespearian sense, he protests too much: the more the truth is made clear to him, the more he resists it, and the more irrationally, artfully and vindictively he does so, precisely because he knows the truth and he knows it has intolerable implications for his conduct, both prospectively and – especially – retrospectively. Outraged protests are a booby trap awaiting anyone who judges self-inflicted problems fairly.

Hence, any group member who persistently draws attention to the self-destructiveness of his fellows – who tries to make them face the truth – is likely to become a frequent target of their anger, and thereby to slip into the role of scapegoat. Self-destructive scapegoaters back each other up in attacking a truth-telling scapegoat partly to secure support for their own attacks on him and partly to gain the advantage of ignoring each other's problems, but also because they do not want their own self-destructiveness to be brought to light. The scapegoat tells the truth, so they call him a liar. As a result, once again, they suffer the outweighing disadvantages of their ongoing self-destructiveness and mutual indifference. And, in so doing, once again they deceive themselves into thinking that they are unified as a group; their subconscious knowledge of their mutual indifference is precisely what consciously unifies them. Here is one of the saddest ironics of scapegoating by groups. In contrast to the scapegoaters – who neglect themselves and each other – the scapegoat genuinely cares about his fellows when he draws attention to the reality of their situation. Indeed, he may slip into the role of scapegoat precisely by pointing out that scapegoating is already occurring within the group; if he speaks up in defence of the group's weak scapegoat, the others may self-deceptively condemn him as well (or instead). But even in this situation, the truth-teller cares about the whole group: by pointing out the truth, his aim is to curb the ongoing dysfunction of the group.

Yet, inadvertently, every scapegoat also has a tendency to make it easier for his scapegoaters to consciously justify their repeated attacks on him. The coarse way in which he is treated dismays him. He feels lonely, and hard done by. As an outcast, he is deprived of whatever support and solace the group is able to afford its members. He starts to wither. And the more he withers the more he hardens. He becomes like an orphaned street urchin who must fight for every privilege. The longer he is scapegoated, the harder he fights, and the harder he fights the more unlikeable he becomes. And all this time – the more he degenerates, the more wretched and coarse and contemptible he becomes – the more the scapegoaters feel certain that their action is justified. The scapegoat is stuck in a positive feedback loop, wherein scapegoating makes him more contemptible, which makes him more likely to be scapegoated, and so on. Any guilt that the scapegoaters feel about their sins or about their treatment of him is thrust further into their subconscious by their increasing conscious certainty that a creature as wretchedly coarse as the scapegoat deserves everything he gets. Even the scapegoat himself may feel some guilt at his coarseness, guilt that weakens him further.

The truth-telling scapegoat, likewise, is trapped in a positive feedback loop of scapegoating and degeneration, but his insistence on the truth puts him in even greater jeopardy. Upon the coarse treatment he receives, he could choose to recant his comments, but more likely – being the sort of person who refuses to deceive himself or others about the truth – he will continue his campaign. His sense of injustice makes him even more determined to seek the understanding of those who have condemned him. But, alas, his insistence on justice only stiffens his sentence. The more vehemently he insists on the truth, the more vehemently his scapegoaters condemn him, the more he suffers and withers and hardens, the less believable he becomes, and the less the truth can prevail. The grip of scapegoating is snake-like: if the scapegoat acquiesces in his treatment, he is trapped in untruth and injustice; if he struggles, he is held there even tighter.

The truth-telling scapegoat starts out powerful enough to think he can make a difference by pointing out the truth – which is to say, genuinely caring about others and their problems – and ends up weakened by that very same effort. Indeed, his persecution may partly stem from others' jealousy of his strength, as though their self-deceptive condemnation of him were thrown like paraffin upon the flame of their persistent ill feeling towards him. Being the sort of person who is strong enough not to flinch from the truth, who is brave enough to speak out against the majority, and who is virtuous enough to do the right thing, can be a huge threat – to others, and, therefore, to oneself. No one likes a show-off.

Is there any way out for the 'permanent' scapegoat? Aside from the group changing its ways, or choosing a new scapegoat – solutions that are beyond his control – his only recourse is to leave the group, like an omega wolf driven off for the last time. However, for the truth-telling scapegoat, another denouement – of sorts – is possible. Sometimes, in his wisdom, he comes to understand that he cannot win, even if he leaves. So he stays, but learns to resist the temptation to point out the elephant in the room; he learns to bite his lip. And the other group members, for their part, come to realise, deep down, that he has something vital to offer them. By way of an uneasy truce, they may occasionally come to him individually when they want advice based on genuine insight. The administering of this advice, however, does not alter the scapegoat's ostracised status, quite the opposite; the scapegoaters are content for the ostracism to continue precisely because they know that the scapegoat's alienated perspective is a vantage point from which the giving of objective advice is possible. The scapegoat becomes like the eponymous hero in Lois Lowry's haunting novel, *The Giver*. The Giver is a wise man who takes on the sufferings and secrets of the people so they can live in a Utopia of ignorance. He is accorded the highest respect of the people, even as they make him an outsider. His knowledge is called upon when asked for; the rest of the time he must keep his counsel or be destroyed.

There are many forms of scapegoating by groups. There are scapegoats who are forced to atone on behalf of a majority whose members are acting in fear of the sanctions of nature; there are scapegoats who, without fair trial, are held directly responsible for natural disasters; and there are scapegoats who are blamed when a group is mutilated not by nature but by endemic dysfunction. All such cases are tragedies of the commons, and typically involve some form of self-deception, whereby scapegoaters turn away from personal responsibility by turning away from self-knowledge. Simultaneously, scapegoaters turn away from reality. To deceive oneself about another person's culpability is always to deceive oneself about reality. Faced by a perilous situation, scapegoaters know just enough to realise how grindingly indifferent the truth is to their well-being. Unable to cope with this realisation, they choose not to scrutinise what they fear, not to exercise personal responsibility, but instead to bury their attention in the self-deception of blame; they choose the wrong kind of empowerment. Some other soul must bear the burden. And, through the ensuing degeneration of the burden-bearer, the scapegoaters' guilt declines by proxy. Sometimes the truth hurts; sometimes it hurts the wrong person.

Still, it is better to be a truth-teller today than centuries ago, when ignorance was more entrenched and violence against scapegoats was an ever-present threat. A truth-teller who, say, gave a dose of reality to a group of witch-hunters – "she couldn't possibly have raised a tempest; the weather doesn't work like *that*" – would quickly have found himself in deep water, perhaps literally. Scapegoating may still be as common today as ever, but thank goodness the apparatus of modern life protects us against the worst excesses of collective mean-spiritedness. We ought to be relieved that we live in such generous times, oughtn't we?

We ought to. Yet many people are complacent about our modern achievements, or, worse, contempt-uous of them. In fulfilling our needs in innovative and synthetic ways, modern life has, ironically, yielded a new and powerful form of scapegoating, one that amalgamates many of the features found in the various past and present instances of scapegoating. Even more ironically, this new form of scapegoating is targeted at anyone who plays a proactive role in shaping or defending the modern world. Moreover, by defining itself against modernity, the new form scapegoating threatens to resurrect some of humanity's very nasty former habits.

Not long before I started writing this book, the Conservative ('Tory') Party was returned to government in Britain with a minority vote but a majority in the Houses of Parliament, following the 2015 general election. Up until polling day, opinion polls had suggested, inaccurately, that the left wing Labour Party was set to win. Commentators attributed the distorted polls to the 'Shy Tory' effect; many conservatives were reluctant to admit, even anonymously, that they intended to vote for a right-of-centre party. Little more was said about this effect, once the pundits were satisfied that they had understood the statistical dynamics of the election, but, when you think about it, the existence of Shy Tories is astounding and worrying. Tories recognise that there is something good to be said for the way our modern world is organised. In a word, they recognise there is something good to be said for capitalism; the system of wealth creation based on individual choice and monetary exchange. They recognise that money is, to use Niall Ferguson's phrase, 'trust inscribed', a near-miraculously effective way of spreading cooperation across vast distances, an accomplishment bolstered by a banking system that leases out money where money is lacking. They recognise that, when individual citizens and organisations are free to work for themselves, exchange the fruits of their labour, and compete with each other, the most useful and efficient practices are promoted, from which everyone in society benefits. They recognise that, compared to any other economic system, capitalism generates – for the many, not just the few – greater prosperity, health, life expectancy, security, peace, art, science, technology, compassion, tolerance and governance. Yet Shy Tories feel the need to apologise for recognising these demonstrable truths, or for playing an active role in shaping the modern world wherein those truths are so evident.

Anti-capitalism is on the rise across the Western world, to the point where capitalists, fearing an angry response, are reluctant to reveal their true colours. Among large swathes of the intelligentsia particularly, it has become taboo to contradict the charge list against capitalism. Greed, inequality, social exclusion, destruction of communities, incivility, crime, educational failure, mental illness, environmental depredation, recession, war: all these scourges allegedly arise from people seeking to enrich themselves and their families through the reciprocal gains of commerce. The more this bizarre causal theory has saturated the zeitgeist, the more the resources of society have been diverted towards government-funded ameliorative programmes. Yet while half a century of steadily increasing state spending has enriched a growing legion of bureaucrats, it has barely dented the problems it was supposed to eradicate; indeed, the problems have worsened. Frustrated by impotence, anti-capitalists have intensified their opposition to what they see as the intensifying malevolence of capitalism, which they assume must be outmanoeuvring their efforts at every turn. In the distorting mirror of self-deceptive righteousness, anti-capitalists perceive the causal arrow back to front. The problems they attribute to capitalism are *caused by*, or at least worsened by, anti-capitalism. And capitalism's own arc towards coarseness – which is ongoing and unmistakable, whichever side of the political spectrum you view it from – is the inevitable consequence of the rise of anti-capitalism; scapegoats, after all, become withered, and hardened, and contemptible.

Perhaps no one emblematises this dynamic better than Margaret Thatcher, the leader of the Conservative Party from 1979 to 1990. Britain's first ever female Prime Minister, Thatcher's death in 2013 was followed, disgracefully, by crowds of socialists burning effigies of her and chanting "ding dong the witch is dead" (and conveniently overlooking the fact that public spending rose under Thatcher's administration), while many commentators on the right acknowledged that her legacy was mixed. Just as her own parliamentary party became rife with corruption during her reign, the British economy became less of a positive influence on people's lives. The story of this continuing decline is the story of scapegoated capitalism.

5

That's a bit rich...

Whether your scepticism be as absolute and sincere as you pretend, we shall learn by and by, when the company breaks up: we shall then see, whether you go out at the door or the window.
– Cleanthes, in David Hume's *Dialogues Concerning Natural Religion*

Following the global depression of 2008, the anti-capitalists who gleefully thought that they were witnessing the end of capitalism were inadvertently paying a back-handed complement to the status quo. "Behold", they were, in effect, saying, "how our global economy based on trade is failing to function! We must replace it with a better system!". They added: "Or next time the crisis will be even worse; capitalism itself will completely collapse!" The subtext of these proclamations is that things get worse when trade breaks down; capitalism is better than a lack of capitalism. Only a belief in an impossible socialist Utopia can subvert the obvious conclusion: capitalism should be cherished not overthrown.

Indeed, you don't need to read between the lines to appreciate that something is awry in the mindset of anti-capitalists; their conduct amply demonstrates their hypocrisy. In 2011, the 'Occupy' movement erected scores of tents outside St Paul's Cathedral in London, in protest against the litany of social and economic problems usually blamed on capitalism. During the occupation, which lasted for months, the Daily Mail cheekily employed an independent thermal imaging company, which established that at night ninety per cent of the tents were... unoccupied. Evidently, the absent protesters were being selective in their rejection of the fruits of capitalism; keeping warm at night using abundantly cheap energy was deemed to be consistent with an overhaul of the system. No less hypocritical are the many anti-capitalists who vigorously complain about supermarkets despite shopping in them on a daily basis. Rather than celebrating the availability of cheap food, tens of thousands of products, and convenient opening hours, anti-capitalists declare supermarkets to be an evil temptation. The same goes, presumably, for the countless other ways in which anti-capitalists are willing beneficiaries of the bounties of modern life.

Anti-capitalism can be found within a diverse range of movements, but perhaps the most widespread article of agreement among anti-capitalists is the urgent need to bring about a more egalitarian society through the planned redistribution of resources by the government. Yet, here again, actions speak louder than words. Many of the people who are involved in the state's attempt to redistribute wealth – including socialist politicians, government bureaucrats and leftist voters – see no contradiction in educating their children privately, in buying expensive houses in the catchment areas of the best state schools, in investing in private healthcare, or in acquiring private health insurance as part of their job remuneration; their desire for equality, it seems, readily gives way to their desire for quality. And I hardly need to mention the numerous 'champagne socialists' who pull in six-figure salaries whether in government or in the wider economy. Redistributing their own wealth (as opposed to that of others) doesn't seem very high on their agenda.

Indeed, if strict equality – as opposed to the inequality which is inevitably caused by the choices made by free individuals wcre really such a desirable thing, you would expect to see anti-capitalists vigorously seeking to expand the quantity and scope of the egalitarian relationships they enjoy with likeminded others. So where are all these exemplary relationships? How many anti-capitalists do you know who enjoy a relationship which is more than superficially based on sharing, apart from within their own family or with a partner? In the 1960s, some anti-capitalists attempted to set up hippy communes, anarchist collectives, free love groups, and so on, and invariably these experiments fell apart following bitter divisions caused by freeloaders who tried to grab more than their fair share (especially their fair share of sex). When today's anti-capitalists sensibly decline to pursue the impossible dream of egalitarianism in their own social relationships, they – hypocritically – display an understanding that what they wish to achieve at the national or international level is undesirable and unrealistic. Everyone is a conservative about what he knows best, observed historian Robert Conquest.

Nor, indeed, are today's anti-capitalists enthusiastic about milder forms of community, for instance teams, societies, charitable organisations, clubs, committees, and so on, in which group members pool only *some* of their resources. In 2010 in Britain, Conservative Prime Minister David Cameron launched his vision for a 'Big Society'. He was influenced by sociologist Robert Putnam who, in his remarkable book *Bowling Alone*, championed the value of 'social capital', i.e. the civilised behaviour and supportive interpersonal bonds often found within groups or communities. (Actually, Putnam distinguishes 'bonding' social capital, which occurs *within* groups, from 'bridging' social capital, which operates *between* members of different groups; by 'social capital' I am referring, as most commentators do, to the bonding kind of social capital.) Areas richer in social capital, Putnam observed, tend to be nicer places to live, with happier and wealthier citizens, better schools, better services and less crime. In championing the power of local communities, Cameron wanted to inspire people to get involved in running local services, to replace overburdened (and burdensome) state-run services with more efficient and effective alternatives. He also hoped that the social capital emerging within engaged local communities would provide much-needed help and support to Britain's most vulnerable citizens, whilst also encouraging all citizens to practise the conscientious and tolerant behaviour required for making a constructive contribution to a group. You might think a mass movement of this kind would be manna from heaven for anti-capitalists, yet they not only ignored Cameron's Big Society rallying cry, they ridiculed it. The very people who, if you take their rhetoric seriously, you would expect to be keen to roll up their sleeves and help to build better communities chose to carp on the sidelines rather than participate. Bizarrely, anti-capitalists showed a reluctance to engage in any activities outside of the purview of modern economic life.

The hypocrisy of anti-capitalists brings to mind a famous passage in philosophy. In his *Dialogues Concerning Natural Religion*, David Hume placed into the mouth of Cleanthes a powerful objection to scepticism (scepticism in philosophy being the view that nothing can be known and there are no grounds for believing one thing rather than another). If you really are a sceptic, Cleanthes says to Philo, then when our conversation is over you will be willing to leave by the upper window rather than by the stairs; according to your scepticism, you will have no reason to favour one over the other. In correctly anticipating that his interlocutor would not endanger himself by departing via the window, Cleanthes was cleverly pointing out that Philo is not *really* a sceptic; he doesn't *really* believe that he has no grounds for believing one thing rather than another. His scepticism is a sham, a rhetorical device designed to project an image of sophistication. Similarly, anti-capitalists who sleep in warm houses rather than tents, shop at supermarkets, pay premiums to live near the best state schools, shun egalitarian relationships, dismiss the importance of social capital, sit on their backsides instead of getting involved in community life, and, generally, condemn capitalism while enjoying its fruits, do not really believe what they are saying, do not really believe that anti-capitalism is a viable alternative to capitalism.

The hypocrisy of anti-capitalists indicates not just sophism but a deeper truth: those who demonise capitalism do not really believe that the supporters of capitalism are exclusively deserving of blame. Even if capitalism were directly responsible for all or some of the sins of which it is accused by anti-capitalists, the day-to-day complicity of those accusers reveals that they are well aware that they share in the responsibility of which they speak. In blaming the supporters of capitalism for capitalism's alleged flaws, in blaming businesses and businesspeople (including bankers) among whom those supporters tend to be concentrated, anti-capitalists are scapegoating a group of individuals, that is, blaming them for an outcome for which everyone should be deemed morally responsible.

(This is assuming that capitalism would indeed deserve 'blame' for any problems that it caused in the course of bringing about its overall positive effect on the well-being of humanity. Consider an analogy: if sweeping a floor caused the broom to get dirty, should the sweeping be *blamed* for the dirty broom?)

The scapegoating of individuals is bad enough when the accused share the blame with their accusers. But, in fact, the blaming of capitalists is more sinister still. The policies advocated and implemented by anti-capitalists do not mitigate but rather cause or worsen the problems that capitalism is accused of causing. Capitalism is therefore blamed not so much for everyone's sins as for sins that belong to its accusers. A casual glance at the soaring trajectories of state spending and social problems suggests as much: the more the government intrudes in our lives, the more shambolic our society becomes. Of course, there is nothing wrong with governance *per se*. Good governance helps uphold the atmosphere of law and order in which trade and cooperation flourishes. The problem is with governance conducted in the name of anti-capitalism. Anti-capitalists arrogantly believe that through planning and controlling society via the state they can engineer outcomes that are fairer and more efficient than those achieved by free people. To this end, anti-capitalists club together in expensive government bureaucracies which seek to subsume more and more of the economy. Proclamations, laws and policies issue forth like a landslide, each lending power to the other, forming a great mass that weighs upon the population, squashing the weakest and most vulnerable especially. Whatever anti-capitalists in government intend to bring about, they mostly cause the opposite effects, whether directly or – by obstructing the efforts of free people – indirectly. It's easier to mess a situation up than get it right – especially if you're trying to control things from afar, from a government office.

For most of us, the negative influence of anti-capitalist governance begins early, in education, and establishes a pattern that continues into many other areas of our lives. Let's consider some of these key areas in turn.

6

The state of education

A self-ordained professor's tongue
Too serious to fool
Spouted out that liberty
Is just equality in school
"Equality", I spoke the word
As if a wedding vow
Ah, but I was so much older then
I'm younger than that now
– Bob Dylan, 'My Back Pages'

In Britain today, around 1.5 million people are employed in the state education system, only 454,900 of whom are teachers. The government spends almost £90 billion annually on education. Among the non-teaching staff, there are around 3000 bureaucrats employed in central government, and thousands more in local authorities.

These 'education' bureaucrats are involved in generating a never-ending stream of strategy reports, targets, data requests, instructions and initiatives. Schools, by law, must respond appropriately to these abstract intrusions, which are backed up by 1500 employees of the government's schools inspectorate, some 400 of whom are on-site inspectors who regularly scrutinise each school in the country. Additionally, one-off inspections are triggered whenever a school attempts to do anything overly independent, such as increasing the number of pupils it admits. Finally, there are meta-inspectors, for want of a better word. In his excellent book *The Welfare State We're In*, James Bartholomew recounts the story of a head teacher who was required to open the school gates to an inspector who inspects the inspectors who inspect the inspectors who inspect the inspectors!

The overarching aim of Britain's state education bureaucracy is to create a system in which as many children as possible get the same opportunities. To this end, over 90 per cent of schools in the UK are 'state schools' – schools funded and managed by the government – and education is compulsory up to the age of 18. Within this broader agenda there are also attempts to micro-manage the lives of specific children. Battalions of educational psychologists, social workers and counsellors are stationed within council offices and schools, prepared to intervene when any child shows signs of falling behind. Such children are 'statemented'; they are allocated a special file upon which is written every possible impediment to their progress, including pseudo-medical conditions such as Attention Deficit Hyperactivity Disorder, Oppositional Defiant Disorder and School Refusal Disorder. Statemented children are closely monitored and given special attention to help them catch up. The name for this overall policy is 'inclusion', alluding to the fact that efforts are made to include all children in education.

At the 'sharp' end of the state's education bureaucracy are, of course, teachers. In order to be deemed 'qualified' (in the eyes of the state), teachers must receive extensive training, to ensure that they have fully absorbed the state's inclusion agenda. Some teachers train on the job, but most attend one of around 70 teacher training colleges. The colleges are staffed by thousands of state-funded educationalists – including philosophers, sociologists, psychiatrists and psychologists – most of whom are 'experts' not in the sense of being experienced teachers but in the sense of knowing lots of theories about inclusion in education. During their training, teachers who take this academic route to qualification spend much more time attending lectures and writing dissertations than actually teaching.

After completing their training, a large number of trainee teachers do not become teachers, or, if they do, 40 per cent drop out within a year of starting. There are over 300,000 non-teaching teachers in the UK, as well as many qualified teachers who are on the payroll but are off sick – a situation much more common in the state sector than in the private sector. What is putting all these expensively trained teachers off?

A National Union of Teachers survey found that within state education the top three reasons cited are (in descending order): 'workload', 'pupil behaviour', and 'government initiatives'. Obviously, the first and third reasons are related. Teachers work too many hours simply because there are too few teachers; too much money is being wasted on government initiatives. These initiatives also ensure that teachers are busy outside of lessons, jumping through an endless series of bureaucratic hoops. Pupils' work must be marked according to time-consuming government formulas that offer scant educational value. Specially formatted reports must regularly be uploaded to awkward computer systems. Further complex data must be collected and stored about statemented children. Forms must be filled in every time any pupil misbehaves or says anything politically incorrect. And teachers themselves are regularly 'evaluated' by the government and rated according to abstract bureaucratic measures. The 'performance management' of teachers seems to have been especially futile given that a recent BBC *Panorama* episode noted that just 18 teachers have been struck off in the last 40 years.

Government initiatives and teachers' workloads are also – no less obviously – related to 'pupil behaviour'. Hampered by bureaucracy, teachers are less able to cultivate relationships of trust, inspiration and support with their pupils, relationships that – of course – make a huge positive difference to the children's behaviour. Moreover, due to staff shortages, class sizes in state schools are often in the thirties, meaning that teachers have a hard time not just building relationships but maintaining order; the latter is true especially of teachers trained by the state. Becoming a qualified teacher is essentially a box-ticking exercise, which – subject knowledge aside – pretty much anyone can complete, whether or not they have the ability to keep a group of children on task. State schools employ far too many uncharismatic cardboard-cut-out teachers who are 'qualified' in the sense that, say, a semaphorist is qualified – knowing all the moves, none of which are relevant to managing a group of children. Meanwhile, suitably knowledgeable people who *are* good at commanding attention – say, former business leaders, ex-military personnel, and many other worldly-wise individuals – are, by default, deemed unqualified to teach, despite the fact that learning the ropes only requires a few weeks in front of a class. In the US, Headmaster Ben Chavis transformed one of the worst schools in California into one of the best. Only a quarter of the teachers he employs are 'certified' by the authorities. He explains: "I don't do no teacher evaluations. All I do is go into a class, and if the kids ain't working, your ass is fired."

The contempt shown by state education towards unqualified teachers is even more ridiculous given that, due to staff shortages and absences, in recent years 'cover' teachers have made up around 4–5 per cent of the teaching force. Cover teachers typically work for employment agencies, are often unqualified, are drafted in at short notice, and know nothing about the subject they are supposed to be covering. They are essentially glorified babysitters, there to do little more than supervise the pupils, for whom the absent teacher sets unchallenging work as a stopgap. For the pupils, a cover teacher is a boon, a chance to kick back and mess about, free of the threat of sanctions – an anonymous outsider has less comeback than an established insider. I know all this firsthand, because a couple of years ago I spent a few months working in numerous schools as a cover teacher through an employment agency, before taking a full-time teaching job for a year and then quitting.

A further impediment to the maintenance of discipline within schools is the state's inclusion agenda. Granted, among the statemented children there are some with severe and genuine developmental problems. These children – who in decades gone by would have received intensive support in 'special' schools – today are often thrown into mainstream education where they learn less, all in the name of inclusion. But that's not the most insulting effect of the policy. Among the statemented children are many whose 'problem' is simply that they misbehave prolifically. Many factors contribute to misbehaviour – the influence of genes, family and peers, among others – but the policy of inclusion insidiously encourages teachers to *excuse* the worst-behaved children. The assumption of the policy is that misbehaviour is inevitable among children who have been ruthlessly "marginalised by our uncaring capitalist society". Naughty children, it follows, have suffered from enough bad luck already; to punish their behaviour would merely add to their 'social exclusion'; what they need is to be included in lessons, regardless. Naturally, the naughtiest children soon assimilate the excuses made on their behalf, with disastrous effect. Instead of being incentivised to rise above their troubles and circumstances, naughty children are left mired in bad behaviour. In turn, other children are dragged in, leading to wider indiscipline, which hampers the learning of whole classes, including children who do not misbehave. Furthermore, the quality of teaching is affected by the lack of discipline. In a desperate effort to capture the attention of unruly pupils, computers are increasingly used in lessons (especially in cover lessons). Children spend valuable learning time scrolling through websites, basically looking at pictures.

The enforcement of discipline is also hampered by the fact that, in the face of excessive bureaucracy, dealing with misbehaviour becomes an afterthought for state schools. And even when beleaguered schools do attempt to impose sanctions on badly behaved children, parents often make official complaints, often with support from the local authorities. Schools that attempt to exclude pupils may face insurmountable legal obstacles.

Meanwhile, in state schools in England around one in 21 pupils are 'persistently absent', that is, they miss more than 20 per cent of lessons. Fear of bullying is a major cause of truancy.

All of this explains why around one in five young adults in England are functionally innumerate, around one in six are functionally illiterate, and around one in six leave secondary school without getting a single C in their GCSE exams. Those statistics are an utterly damning indictment of the quality of state education, of the approximately 10,000 hours of education state school children receive at a cost of around £11,000 per year per pupil. This cost is only around £2000 less than the average annual amount spent per head on Britain's private school pupils, whose attainment is notoriously higher; a study published this year suggested that, at age 16, private school pupils are two years ahead of state school pupils. Indeed, private schools do better than state schools the world over, even when factors such as the wealth and background of the pupils' parents are taken into account.

Invariably, anti-capitalists will respond by arguing that one in five or six is better than... something worse. State schools, the argument goes, do a heroic job in difficult circumstances, circumstances caused by capitalism. I have no doubt that many teachers do a heroic job. However, a cursory knowledge of the history of state education in Britain reveals that, far from being the enemy of learning, free markets actually work wonders *within* education.

We are so steeped in the notion that the government should provide universal, compulsory education, few of us have any inkling that there is an alternative. In *The Welfare State We're In*, Bartholomew recounts some important lessons from history. In the middle of the nineteenth century, before the state got involved in education, school attendance was growing rapidly, as was literacy. By 1870, when minister W. E. Forster passed a law enabling the state to fill in 'the gaps', more than 95 per cent of children were regularly attending school. It is hard to determine with complete accuracy the literacy levels at that time, but when the last generation of students who were unaffected by the Forster Act had reached the average marriage age, over 90 per cent of spouses were signing the marital register with their name – a measure historians use as a proxy for literacy. In other words, the best available evidence suggests that, before the state intervened, the Victorian education system was producing a 90 per cent rate of literacy in young people.

The Victorian public was demanding education, and the open economy was supplying it, effectively and innovatively. The aspirations of all kinds of people, young and old, were catered to by a huge variety of independent learning establishments and educators: Dame schools, Ragged Schools, Mutual Improvement Societies, Literary and Philosophical Institutes, Sunday Schools, Factory Schools, Quaker Schools, and Freelance Lecturers who travelled from town to town. Compared to today, parents had much greater control over the hours and type of schooling that their children received, and this control created a close link between schools and communities, as did the fact that parents naturally showed an interest in what they were paying for; in turn, the children were motivated to take their education seriously. This was especially true of working class families, who, by virtue of being poor, valued education all the more.

From the schools' perspective, there was money to be made in providing affordable education to the poor, and so it was. Today we are familiar with Charles Dickens's caricatures of schooling in Victorian England: *Nicholas Nickleby* and *Hard Times* paint a picture of grim exploitation. But these are works of fiction! In 1852, Dickens returned to a school that he had previously witnessed struggling in its early days, and gave the following factual account: 'I found it quiet and orderly, full, lighted with gas, well whitewashed, numerously attended, and thoroughly established.' To appreciate why these standards were not uncommon, you again have to consider the motives of the people involved in education in the nineteenth century. Choosy customers led to competition between commercial educators, and this drove standards up. And many Victorian schools were charities, funded by philanthropists and run by educators who were in it for the love of it. Also notable is the fact that the bestowal of charity leads to gratitude, whereas the bestowal of rights can lead to a toxic sense of entitlement. Though most charitable schools – on principle – required the poorest parents to pay a small fee, the parents and their children would have been acutely aware of the opportunity they had been generously given.

Forster didn't intend for his 1870 Act to impact upon the great flowering of freely chosen education that was taking place in the nineteenth century. But impact it did, as the state began its long advancement into the upbringing of the nation's children. Independent schools suffered first; they not only faced competition with free or heavily subsidised state schools but were forced to pay rates to the government. Many people had made great sacrifices to run independent schools, only to see their efforts wiped out, or swallowed up when the state took over. Only the richest independent schools catering for the richest customers survived.

At the time, some commentators correctly foresaw the negative consequences of state education. In his 1850 book *Education Best Promoted by Perfect Freedom, not by State Endowments*, Edward Baines warned that the death of independent schools would strip from education the influence of philanthropic individuals and community organisations such as churches. In turn, Baines warned against undermining the 'happy social influence' of learning establishments in which the middle and upper classes were cooperating with the working classes. He also saw that the state would undermine the influence of parents within education; not only would they value less what was compulsory, but even if they did remain interested they would be less able to exercise control over their children. He saw that head teachers would be undermined, their decision-making powers – for example, in teacher recruitment – curtailed by officialdom. He saw that the government, with its inefficiency, inflexibility and lack of innovation, would be a poor substitute for a thriving market in education.

Baines was right. And he was right to hint that the biggest casualties of the state's clumsy attempts to educate poor people would be poor people themselves.

Today, state schools in the poorest areas contain a dysfunctional mix of hopelessly non-academic children and hopelessly academic children. In the middle decades of the twentieth century, non-academic children were taught the three Rs then permitted to focus on vocational skills. But in our enlightened modern era, these children are forced onto an academic trajectory, where they miss out on appropriate learning opportunities, and become disillusioned, and disruptive. In turn, the disruption hampers the learning of academically talented poor children. According to recent research, children from the poorest backgrounds are less likely to reach the highest levels of academic achievement today than in 1970.

One remaining way for clever poor children to get ahead is to attend a 'grammar school' – a state school that selects the highest-performing children from within the state system and provides them with an academic education to rival that of private schools. However, grammar schools in Britain were shut down in droves in the 1960s and 70s. 'I'm going to destroy every fucking grammar school in England and Wales and Northern Ireland', said Tony Crosland, Labour Education Secretary from 1965 to 1967. This act of sabotage was predicated on the notion that state education should give all children the same opportunities. But it hasn't turned out that way. A study by the Centre for Social Justice found a near-perfect correlation between the quality of the results in state schools and the poverty of the area in which state schools are situated. The dead hand of state education often means death to the ambitions of the poor; in 2012, a report found that social mobility in Britain is the lowest in the Western world.

Tellingly – and poignantly – in Britain in recent years the number of parents trying to enrol their children in a state school whose catchment area they do not live in has been at historically unprecedented levels. There has been about one appeal for every ten state school admissions. Not only do these appeals waste time and money (it would be far more efficient and sensible to allow people to choose which school they send their children to, as per capitalism), but the appeal system exacerbates inequality in education. In the rarefied bureaucratic milieu that determines the fate of each schoolchild, the middle class parents – articulate, savvy, well connected – are likely to wield more influence than the poor parents. A system in which grammar schools enabled poor children to escape from poverty has been replaced, largely, with a system in which middle class children are being evacuated from the worst schools.

Thankfully, at the time of writing, Britain's Tory government has taken steps to restore some sanity to state education (to the extent that any state bur-eaucracy can be made sane: sadly, abolishing state education altogether is electorally impossible). A few months ago, Education Secretary Nicky Morgan announced that England was to get its first new grammar school in fifty years. Her predecessor, Michael Gove, passed laws enabling existing state schools to opt out of local authority control; the new 'academy' status would enable these schools to make their own decisions to a larger degree. Simultaneously, Gove permitted the founding of 'free schools', new schools funded by the state but run by parents or community groups. All this is in keeping with

Cameron's Big Society vision, and, indeed, is supported by a Programme for International Student Assessment report that showed that autonomy is good for schools the world over. Greater parental and community involvement in schools generates social capital, which is particularly important in education; it takes a village to raise a child, after all. Under the positive influence of engaged communities, schoolchildren can be steered away from the *Lord of the Flies*-style peer socialisation that flourishes in the disciplinary vacuum created by state-run schools.

Yet the prospect of reform for the education system in Britain remains severely limited. Gove was replaced by Nicky Morgan after making too many enemies. His determination to create free schools and academies was met by fierce opposition – including vitriolic personal abuse – from educationalists, academics, teaching unionists, bureaucrats, politicians and left wing journalists, that is, anyone with a vested interest in the continuation of anti-capitalist governance within the education sector. Especially unpopular was Gove's ruling that free schools and academies could recruit 'unqualified' teachers – such as myself. (Moreover, since this chapter was written, Morgan herself has been thwarted in her efforts to impose academy status on every British school; apparently, even the government can't stop people from craving dependence on the government.) Gove described education's huge anti-capitalist lobby as the 'blob', referring to the Hollywood B-movie in which a protoplasmic alien subsumes everything in its path, growing and growing unstoppably. As long as the blob remains ensconced within state education, lasting change will be hard to effect. And worse, the reach of the blob – of anti-capitalist governance – extends way beyond education, into many other areas of our lives.

7

The welfare racket

Every town and village should know their own paupers ... and assist them. But as to ... strange beggars they ought not to be born with.

– Martin Luther

Each year in Britain, around £220–250 billion is spent on state-run welfare provision. Excluding pensions from that figure, around £110 billion is spent on benefits. More than 20 million families in Britain now receive some kind of state benefit. Nearly half of those families receive over half of their income in government subventions, to which the average earner in Britain contributes around £2135 of his annual salary. The Department of Work and Pensions, which administrates the welfare state, employs around 90,000 people. Additionally, there are 433 local authorities in Britain, each of which employs scores or hundreds of people in welfare roles. As Theodore Dalrymple has wryly observed: 'One man's poverty is another man's employment opportunity.'

Whatever the anti-capitalists say, welfare is very, very big business, especially in Britain, which now has roughly 7 per cent of the world's total welfare spend. Adjusted for inflation, and excluding pensions, the annual UK welfare spend has climbed to more than three times its 1980 levels, and has plateaued under the current Conservative administration. There are many reasons for the overall rise. For many years, the major political parties competed with each other in their promises of generosity ('I will give you more money' provides a sturdier electoral platform than 'I owe you nothing'). In turn, the growing catchment of the welfare state has led to an increase in the complexity of welfare bureaucracy. Today, the state hands out money according to various categories, including child benefit, housing benefit, unemployment benefit, income support, winter fuel payments, child credits, working tax credits, council tax benefit, incapacity benefit, and carer's allowance. Similarly, within each category the eligibility criteria and the payments have become fiendishly complicated. The application form for tax credits, for instance, comes with 24 pages of advisory notes. Recently, the government has tried to reduce all this complexity by trialing 'universal credit', a welfare category that amalgamates six others. But the overall trend has been towards a massive administrative burden, which has added to the cost of the welfare state. In the long run, government bureau-cracies have a tendency to expand, unchecked by market forces. As bureaucrats have sought to increase the sizes of their fiefdoms, the cost of welfare has soared.

But there is another, far more troubling, reason for the increase in welfare spending: *the welfare state has failed.* At first sight, the reason doesn't make sense. How can failure have thrived so extensively? A closer inspection reveals the alarming explanation. The more the welfare state has grown, the more it has fostered the kind of impoverishment – financial, physical and mental – for which welfare is touted as the answer. State welfare is a racket.

When I was a child, a classmate once confessed to me that his dad, a builder, deliberately pulled tiles off the roof whenever he was fixing the gutters on his customers' houses. He would then ask for more money to fix the roof. I'm not sure if his scam had any further iterations. Did he, say, smash some windows while he fixed the roof then demand more money to install new glass? I doubt he could have got away with profiting from causing repeated damage. And yet the welfare state has prospered for half a century through inflicting harm upon harm on British society.

The welfare state has grown in keeping with its tendency to incentivise citizens to behave in such a way that they qualify for the receipt of benefits. Obviously, not everyone deliberately tries to receive benefits, but the temptation is there. In the first place, people face an incentive to begin receiving benefits, after which they face an incentive to continue receiving them. Benefits are allocated on the basis of *need*, which means, on the whole, that the most self-destructive applicants have an advantage over the most self-reliant. In other words, the more recklessly a person lives, the more he or she is likely to qualify for benefits. By encouraging more and more people to behave self-destructively, and then encouraging them to perpetuate that behaviour, the welfare state has built and consolidated its client base.

In saying this, I am of course distinguishing between the deserving poor and the undeserving poor. Anti-capitalists hate this distinction, because it divides their compassion, and therefore diminishes their self-regard. To anyone else, however, it is screamingly obvious that sometimes people bring about their own suffering. In failing to recognise as much, the welfare state compromises deserving claimants, and encourages the self-infliction of harm.

A clear illustration of such encouragement can be seen in the effects of unemployment benefit. The name is, unintentionally, a giveaway: when unemployment benefit is high it has a tendency to promote unemployment. Between 1945 and 1970, the annual unemployment rate in Britain averaged roughly 2 per cent, and never rose higher than 3.1 per cent. The value of the dole was low and unemployment remained low. But following a succession of increases in unemployment benefit (compared to the value of average wages), in 1955, 1958, 1961, 1963 and 1965, the unemployment rate jaggedly climbed to 13 per cent in 1982 and has bounced around above roughly 5 per cent ever since. As James Bartholomew puts it: 'Mass unemployment has been made a permanent feature of life.' The slight delay in the effect of those increases in the value of unemployment benefit can be explained by the amount of time it took for the new laws to become well known. But the lesson is clear enough: the incentives to keep a job or find a job are reduced when people are assured a good income from not working. The same goes for the incentives to start a business. Growing a business is a great route out of poverty, yet generous unemployment benefit stifles the motivation of would-be entrepreneurs. When you can receive a guaranteed income without getting off the sofa, the risks and rigours of running a business seem less attractive.

So, too, do the potential rewards of work. Unemployment benefit can induce a sense of apathy, which blinds recipients to their prospects for a better life. Apathy is a double-edged sword; the airy satisfaction of being given money for nothing also comes with a sense of hopelessness. Having nothing to do all day is terrible for the soul. Long-term unemployed people are more likely to smoke, drink and take drugs. They are more likely to be angry and to commit crimes. They are more likely to be unhappy, neurotic and to commit suicide. Working provides social interaction and a sense of status; being out of work brings isolation and a sense of worthlessness. In offering citizens an incentive to eschew paid work, the welfare state fosters apathy and its dreadful downsides.

Unemployment also causes physical illness, due to the malign effects of stress on health. This goes some way to explaining why the number of people on disability benefits exploded in recent decades. But the current Conservative administration believes there is more to the story, and has caused widespread consternation by attempting to reform the disability benefits system so as encourage hundreds of thousands of claimants to return to work. According to recent statistics, around 1 in 14 working-age people in Britain receives some form of disability benefit. No doubt, many of these people are unfortunate and deserving. But of the approximately 3 million disability benefits claimants in Britain, it is equally doubtless that many have been incentivised to develop or perpetuate self-inflicted health conditions. For instance, around 12,000 people in Britain receive government support because they are too fat to work, while over a million people receive disability benefits for mental health issues, in two thirds of those cases for depression or anxiety. Then there are the 75,000 drug addicts or alcoholics who receive disability benefits (for their habit, as it were). Granted, some of these fat or depressed or addicted people are severely ill. Others, however, are simply living badly and being rewarded for it by the state.

Another factor accounting for the explosion of incapacitated jobless people in Britain has been the vulnerability of the system to fraud. Only time will tell if the current reforms will change that. In 2012, 150,960 claimants fell into the category of "Back Pain / Other / Precise Diagnosis Not Specified". Back pain is a condition which is no easier to diagnose objectively than depression or anxiety. In effect, huge sums of money are handed out each year on the say-so of the recipients – a recipe for abuse of the system. Indeed, fraud is a problem across the whole of the welfare state. Two of the most common kinds of fraudulent claim involve people living with a partner while claiming to be the sole occupant of a dwelling, and people working while claiming to be unemployed or unable to work. A government report estimated that fraudulent claims in 2012 cost the taxpayer £1.2 billion. Then there are the added costs of trying to combat benefit fraud, a task that is in any case near-futile: the state cannot track all benefit claimants all the time.

I hesitate to cite the problem of fraud, because it detracts from another real problem, which is the unreasonable nature of many 'legitimate' welfare claims. Consider the following example. In one of the various 'day jobs' I have held over the years, I worked with a man who, when he was at school, was statemented with 'Asperger syndrome' – a condition which involves difficulty in social relationships and communication. Asperger's comes in degrees, and my colleague had it very mildly, if at all. The mildness of his problem was illustrated by the fact that *he was the customer services officer for the company we worked for* – not exactly a job you can perform if your social skills aren't up to scratch, and, indeed, he was good at his job. Meanwhile, however, he received income support and housing benefit from the government, based on his childhood diagnosis of Asperger's. He lived, rent free, thanks to his housing benefit, in a flat in one of the most expensive parts of town. His live-in partner was registered as his 'carer', and received extra income for this role, despite the fact that both of them had jobs. Every day at work, my colleague showed me photographs on his iPhone of the things he and his partner were spending their money on: five-star restaurants, a two-week holiday in Mauritius, a £500 3D flat screen TV, a 'star in the sky' (costing just £27.99, as a romantic present for Valentine's Day – because "stars are for eternity") – and much more. Most of this was being paid for by other people.

I pointed out to my colleague that he was, in effect, spending some of *my* money on fripperies, and I suggested that there are undoubtedly plenty of disability benefits claimants who need the money more than he does. He wasn't sympathetic. It was the government's money to give away, and he was entitled to it, and that was that. In fact, my colleague isn't the only recipient of social security to develop a somewhat anti-social attitude. By enticing people into the trap of joblessness, apathy, fraudulence or frivolity, the welfare state damages people's morality. Free money can discourage citizens from understanding the true value of hard work. Among welfare recipients, there are many who display no gratitude; rather, they have a sense of entitlement towards their benefits. They think of rights, not of responsibilities. They think not of making do and mending, but of spending. They are discouraged from saving, because savings might jeopardise their eligibility for welfare. The 'consumerist' attitude that is bemoaned by anti-capitalists is caused, in part, by our welfare culture.

Perhaps one of the most sorrowful impacts of state welfare on the morality of citizens can be seen in Britain's high levels of teenage pregnancy and family breakdown. Almost a quarter of British children are now raised by lone parents – the highest figure in Western Europe. The welfare state encourages lone parenting, which, in turn, leads to step-parenting, with the higher risk of child abuse that entails. Before conceiving, mothers and fathers alike are assured that the state will pay to raise every child, come what may. Under this provocation, mothers not only exercise less restraint in their sexual liaisons, but indeed are positively encouraged to conceive; a baby might inspire a favoured boyfriend to stick around, and, if not, will provide a permanent, guaranteed income. Fathers, meanwhile, are given the opportunity to spawn offspring at will, confident in the knowledge that the state will pick up the tab. For men and women, state welfare is a powerful stimulant to sexual irresponsibility. This is true even within marriages. When spouses receive money from the government *simply for having children*, the cost of separation, and therefore of having affairs and mistreating each other, is mitigated, and more likely to be considered worth paying.

All this is bad enough without the state exacerbating the situation by gathering welfare claimants together in state-run housing estates, where the misbehaviour and misery of Britain's most misbehaving and miserable citizens is compounded by their mutual association. There are around 4.1 million social homes in Britain, and 3.3 million of their inhabitants receive housing benefit. The word 'deprived' is commonly used to describe the nation's worst council estates, but 'depraved' would be more accurate. Stairways and corridors are spattered with urine and faeces. Discarded needles and other drug-taking paraphernalia are scattered on the ground. Graffiti covers the walls. Prostitutes trade out of their homes. Gangs of youths loiter, trapped in a perpetual state of cosseted adolescent resentment. Crime and violence are common, as is religious radicalism, which feeds terrorism. Many council estates are *de facto* no-go areas for the police, partly due to a lack of resources, and partly due to a lack of intent. Just as the welfare state represents an extension of the educational theory of inclusion into the lives of adults – where once again it excuses and rewards misbehaviour – inclusion has also crept into the legal system, leading to criminals being treated leniently because supposedly their unlawful behaviour is a passive response to their social circumstances. When you also take into account the absurd levels of bureaucracy involved in modern police work, it is hardly surprising that police officers today are barely distinguishable from social workers. Of course, the real effect of police lenience is that law-abiding poor people are chronically tormented by the crime and anti-social behaviour of their neighbours.

The decadence of council estates reflects the bad designs of anti-capitalists in the architectural sense as well as the ideological sense. The Piggeries in Liverpool, Red Road in Glasgow, the Broadwater Farm Estate in London, the Manor Estate in Sheffield, the Divis Flats in Belfast, the Noble Street Estate in Newcastle: government-built dwellings are usually aesthetic abominations that can hardly inspire a sense of aspiration in residents. State housing often fails functionally, too. Huge apartment blocks sometimes have front entrances for the use of a thousand people, and this undermines residents' (already flimsy) sense of ownership of their territory, and, by making it hard for them to know who really does and doesn't live there, hampers social capital. Residents feel isolated, out of control, and nihilistic. No wonder council estates become such a mess, socially and physically.

As for councils, they, too, often fail to keep their properties well maintained; naturally, people who own their own homes are more conscientious about maintenance than office workers managing distant dwellings. Indeed, the ultimate fate of the government's ugly and neglected housing blocks is usually demolition – by the government. In his brilliant book *No They Can't*, the American broadcaster and libertarian polemicist John Stossel concludes by describing the various ways in which he would slash the US federal budget. He would, for instance, completely eliminate the Department of Housing and Urban Development. His reason? 'They build horrible housing projects and then blow them up.'

Anti-capitalists will invariably respond to these points by insisting that the state provision of welfare, including housing, for poor people is better than the alternative of doing nothing. The existence of a needy underclass, so the argument goes, is caused not by welfare but by capitalism, by the capitalistic greed that corrupts the morals of poor people and leads to insufficient generosity and solicitousness among the affluent. It is difficult enough to maintain this argument in the face of the evidence of the present, but even more difficult in the face of history. Before the welfare state, the poor had better welfare and needed less welfare, and people were more charitable – all of which is documented once again in Bartholomew's enlightening book.

Social security in some form or another has probably been around for as long as people have been around, but the first stirrings of state influence within welfare occurred in the mid-sixteenth century. The impetus came, indirectly, from Henry VIII's failure to secure Papal sanction for his divorce with Catherine of Aragon, who had failed to provide the monarch with a male heir. Henry systematically stripped England's Catholic monasteries of their wealth and power, and founded the Church of England to replace them. But the monasteries were the principal source of welfare at that time, so their demise caused a crisis in vagrancy and poverty. In response, Henry's government inaugurated the Poor Laws, according to which local mayors and governors were required to secure and disseminate charitable donations from parishioners. In 1563 the rules were tightened by Henry's successor Elizabeth I, under whom welfare payments became mandatory. The Poor Laws then remained fairly stable for almost 300 years.

In 1834, Parliament commissioned a report into the effect of the Poor Laws on Britain. The report found that spending on welfare had risen almost fivefold during the last half century, and had wrought the same problems as we see today – dependency, idleness, fraud, sexual irresponsibility, and debauchery. The report's authors, led by Edwin Chadwick, recommended draconian reductions in welfare combined with the universal adoption of the harshest measures found amongst the various parishes: for instance, all benefits should be scrapped outside 'poor houses', in which beggars, vagrants and general unfortunates were to be corralled and put to work.

Also influential at the time was a pastor called Thomas Chalmers. He observed that charities large enough to be run from central offices – i.e. away from local areas of need – tended to foster the downsides of welfare to a greater degree than smaller, locally based administrations. He insisted that in his Glasgow parish money should only ever be given out sparingly and temporarily, while personal contact with those who sought support should be administered lavishly. The Deacons under his charge were to enquire very closely into the lives of all claimants. Was work available? How had they come to need assistance? Did they have family who could help? Chalmers opposed any form of centrally run welfare, including state welfare. As he explained: 'There is a charm in locality most powerfully felt by every man who tries it ... who has personally attached himself to a manageable portion of the civic territory.' He added: 'There is a far greater sufficiency among the lower classes of society than is generally imagined; and our first impressions of their want and wretchedness are generally by far too much aggravated: nor do we know a more effectual method of reducing these impressions than to cultivate a closer acquaintance with their resources, and their habit, and their whole domestic economy.'

The government of the day passed the recommendations of the 1834 report. What followed was a period of welfare austerity, and a flourishing of the 'Victorian virtues' of self-reliance, hard work, and charity. Explosive economic growth – unparalleled since – followed too, accompanied by a spirit of generosity also unparalleled since. The average family of the time donated 10 per cent of its earnings to good causes (compared to today's figure of 1 per cent); working class families donated too. As Bartholomew notes: 'It is hard for us to imagine now how large charity loomed in people's lives in the late nineteenth century.' It is also hard, seemingly, for modern Britons to imagine how the virtue of self-reliance could exist alongside the virtue of generosity. But the connection is not so strange when you think about it: self-reliant people are the ones capable of helping others.

Following the 1834 report, another important cultural shift took place, one that is perhaps even more alien to us today. People spontaneously formed 'Friendly Societies', community-based insurance schemes that members paid into on a regular basis and drew from in times of personal hardship. Although such schemes had been around for centuries, they became so popular in Victorian times that by the late nineteenth century there were nearly 30,000 Friendly Societies in Britain. Almost everyone lived near numerous such organisations and could choose which to join. By the early twentieth century, Edward Brabrook, the Chief Registrar of Friendly Societies, declared that only 'a kind of residuum' of people went without some kind of freely chosen social insurance.

The great thing about Friendly Societies was that they embodied Thomas Chalmers's philosophy of localised, personalised welfare. They were run by their members, for their members. They fostered a sense of team spirit, through regular meetings and events. They required certain standards of behaviour from their members, and if those standards weren't met people were excluded. Many Friendly Societies also hosted regular lectures, to encourage self-improvement; likewise, the demands of cooperating and negotiating with other members encouraged positive traits such as patience, tolerance, trust and give-and-take – in a word, civility. There was also a natural, spontaneous egalitarianism found within Friendly Societies; a builder, say, could hold a more senior role than a barrister, and within some memberships the position of Chair was rotated, so that everyone would have a chance to experience leadership. With so much social capital emerging within Friendly Societies, they were far less prone to abuse than today's welfare state. Most members simply did not want to defraud or burden their fellows, whom they respected and were respected by. And, as per Chalmers's intuition, the scrutiny that members naturally placed on each other's claims discouraged fraud and encouraged claimants to recover their self-reliance as soon as possible.

Alas, Friendly Societies were, in a way, victims of their own success. Seeking to emulate that success – while also seeking to placate a growing Marxist lobby – the British government of 1911, led by Lloyd George of the Liberal Party, implemented a National Insurance scheme. Support for the scheme came also from William Churchill, then a cabinet minister, who had been influenced by the impressive social organisation he had encountered on a recent trip to Germany. George and Churchill had no intention of undermining the existing Friendly Societies, but that's what happened. The national scheme, being compulsory, disincentivised people from investing their money and time in Friendly Societies; what was the point, when the government was now providing a (supposedly) equivalent service? Similarly, what was the point in being charitable when the government was (supposedly) already doing everything that needed to be done for poor people? Friendly Societies and the charitable impulse collapsed as the welfare state grew (and, not uncoincidentally, the Great Depression followed, which amplified the clamour for more state welfare). When, in 1942, William Beveridge published his famous government report on 'Social Insurance and Allied Services', half a million copies flew off the shelves, despite the fact that Beveridge was an admirer of Friendly Societies, and despite the fact that his recommendations ultimately led to state benefits becoming tougher to access and, due to inflation, lower in value. It mattered not. The public's enthusiasm for national welfare schemes ensured that, roughly a decade later, the welfare state resumed its precipitous growth in size and generosity.

Today, the lessons of Chalmers and the Friendly Societies have been almost forgotten: money, not personal attention, is handed out generously by the modern welfare state. A handful of Friendly Societies remain (for example, Kingston Unity, Liverpool Victoria, and the Exeter Friendly Society) but now *they* are the residuum; as are the Victorian virtues of self-reliance, hard work and charity; and as is economic growth. Indeed, the welfare state is ignorant not just of past wisdom but of modern wisdom too. Contemporary psychology has corroborated what the

Victorians knew (and what common sense knows), namely that the encouragement of independence requires an appropriate response to people's emotional and psychological needs; merely doling out money has the effect of being both dismissive of people's real needs and permissive of their indulgences and mistakes – the worst of both worlds. Like flippant father like wayward son, the welfare state makes its mistakes over and over.

The story of state welfare – of blundering state intervention crushing the spontaneous, effective, cooperative efforts of free people – is mirrored in the history of state housing. Victorian times saw a surge in commercial house building, which ensured that a tripling of the population of Britain's cities was accompanied by a level of supply more than adequate to meet the new demand; the number of people per household declined. But under Lloyd George's government in the early twentieth century, the Housing and Town Planning Act sanctioned the building of tens of thousands of homes by local authorities and by state-subsidised private builders. 'Slums', usually consisting of rows of terraced houses, were forcibly cleared and replaced by newer housing stock. Some of the dwellings that were replaced were undoubtedly grim, but by no means all of them. Considering the desirability of Victorian terraces today – many of which are among the most expensive places to live in the country – one wonders how many perfectly good streets were destroyed by the state over the last century. Even worse, slum clearance also meant the displacement of people. Extended families were separated from each other, communities were destroyed, social capital waned. Networks of local support were smashed apart just as much as bricks and mortar.

In housing as in welfare, the latter half of the twentieth century saw an acceleration of the state's role. In the 1960s, Harold Wilson's Labour government enthusiastically embraced the trend, still lamentably present today, for erecting huge concrete residential state tower blocks. In 1965, rent controls – which had been around for half a century but had been loosened under the previous (Conservative) government – were extended and tightened, and this, as ever, had the unintended side effect of discouraging builders from building; the enforcement of low rents meant that commercial companies struggled to make a profit from construction. In turn, the ensuing lack of new homes supplied a quasi-legitimacy to the government's role in housing; if there weren't enough homes, then the government needed to do more – right? Also in the mid-1960s, National Building Regulations were passed for the first time. And, over the years, more and more housing market regulations followed – including stricter planning laws, swingeing property taxes, housing safety regulations, and new green belt areas – which further limited the viability of commercial house building, and supplied further quasi-legitimacy to state interventions in housing.

Today, the government has a regulatory stranglehold on housing, and inevitably house prices (and rents) have soared to historically unprecedented levels. This is good for the rich homeowners, and bad for everyone else: quite the opposite of what the anti-capitalists intended. Every year, politicians – of both stripes – talk bombastically of redoubling government house building efforts, apparently unaware (as are the majority of voters) of the fact that state-controlled industries are rarely, if ever, as productive as free markets. Money is taken from the taxpayer's pocket and spent, in the name of 'housing', on grossly inefficient bureaucratic practices at the local and national level – on yet more strategy reports, initiatives, databases, and so on. Far fewer houses get built by the government than would be built if the markets were permitted to work their magic, allowing builders to build and sell at prices at which buyers could afford to buy, thus benefitting both parties.

The situation isn't helped – to put it mildly – by Britain's steadily increasing level of net migration, with the population swelling by hundreds of thousands each year (last year's net migration figure of 330,000 – with 636,000 people incoming – was the highest ever recorded). Anyone who has the audacity to point out the discrepancy between our perennially sluggish government-controlled housing sector and the increasing number of people who need homes in Britain is immediately labelled a racist by anti-capitalists.

Obviously there's nothing wrong with immigration *per se*. Immigrants are some of the best people around. But in the current housing crisis, held fast by the state, Britain's soaring level of net migration is causing desperate overcrowding, which is hurting poor people above all.

And obviously it is true that there are some xenophobic people in the lower echelons of society. But in deliberately blurring xenophobic arguments against immigration and economic arguments against excessive net migration, anti-capitalists insult reasonable poor people and trounce their rational concerns.

No wonder extreme political organisations of all kinds – left, right and religious – with their promises of power through means other than reason, are growing in popularity.

Such is the racket that is anti-capitalism, as exemplified by state welfare and state housing. First destroy: destroy Friendly Societies, the work ethic, people's sense of self-reliance, people's generosity of spirit, people's homes, communities, and so on. Then promise to replace what you destroyed. Then fail, expensively, repeatedly, disastrously. And vilify anyone who dares to make a rational case against the politically correct nostrums of the day.

Life imitates art

Uncannily, at this exact juncture, I have found out that I will need to vacate my home. I currently – for the next three days, anyway – live in a detached out-building in the garden of a property in Cambridge, England. Whilst my dwelling is heated more than adequately, it doesn't have a toilet or kitchen, but I have access to the facilities in the main house, which is twenty yards away, through the garden. In many ways, I love where I live; it affords me peace and quiet and privacy, which are priceless to a writer.

Well, actually they're not priceless, but most writers don't make much money; I can't afford the rent that a fully equipped detached property of this kind would fetch. The relatively low rent I pay far outweighs the relative inconvenience of having to walk to the main house to use the facilities. In fact, the 'inconvenience' is mostly quite fun – like a permanent camping trip! And it's nothing I haven't experienced before. When I lived in King's College, Cambridge, while completing my PhD, I lived in a historic court in a room that was located more than twenty yards away from a toilet. I had to walk through an open-air corridor to access the bathroom.

Anyway, it turns out that my current home is illegal. There is a law against 'Beds in Sheds' in

Britain, to deter supposedly unscrupulous landlords from letting out supposedly sub-par housing to immigrants. The government 'cares' about poor people, such as myself, and in a few days will inspect my home – presumably following a tip-off by a neighbour – after which I will be moved on, supposedly in my own interests.

Let's get a few things straight. I *choose* to live in the garden room, because it is in my interests. My landlord chooses to rent it to me, because it is in his interests. He cannot afford to fully equip the room, because this would require expensive planning permission. My landlord is himself an immigrant, and poor. He has – entrepreneurially – found a way to ease the housing crisis in Cambridge, and has mightily helped a writer like me (not to mention a succession of previous tenants who lived happily in the room). I cannot vouch for the others, but I certainly haven't caused any inconvenience to the neighbours; I live a monkish existence as a writer.

Yet, on Thursday someone who works for the local authority, who is being paid out of a multimillion-pound government fund for 'cracking down' on Beds in Sheds, is due to turn up at my home, enter it against my will, shake their head, and, with the full force of the law, demand that I vacate it. Are we living in a democracy or a totalitarian state? In the last few years, according to a Daily Mail article, over 40,000 such inspections have taken place, and 3000 landlords are now facing 'further enforcement or prosecution'. Fines can be as high as £5000, and local authorities have the powers to destroy 'unsuitable' dwellings, while the government is creating a database of landlords who break the Beds in Sheds rule.

Obviously, neither myself nor any other poor person is a beneficiary of the rule. I don't (presently) want to live elsewhere. I certainly don't want the government to tell me where I can and cannot live – not when I am living on private land with the permission of the owner, and using my earned income to fulfil the financial arrangement I entered into willingly. So why does the rule exist? Government Minister for housing, Brandon Lewis, has complained of 'rogue landlords' who are 'creating a shadow housing market'. Now we're getting to the heart of it. It's the same old persecution of capitalists – in this case, all those nasty landlords who want to profit from their tenants. And it's the same old welfare racket, in a slightly different guise. The 'shadow housing market' cannot be allowed to exist because this would relieve pressure on housing; it would supply homes to people who need homes, and this would mean that we don't need government bureaucrats to provide us with homes. The bureaucrats are dismantling the shadow housing market just as my friend's dad dismantled the roofs of his customers. Lower income rent-payers like myself are being forced into the government-regulated housing market where the rents (and tax revenues) are higher, which both exacerbates the housing crisis and swells the government's coffers. From these outcomes it follows – supposedly – that the government should 'do something' to house poor people, the very same poor people, like me, who the government is systematically evicting from their own freely chosen homes.

I'll have to move out of my house in the next few days, to protect myself and my landlord from the benevolent strictures of the state. I wasn't planning to live in an outbuilding forever, and I'm sure that no poor person or immigrant ever plans to do so. But I'm now less likely to escape from my economic predicament, due to the economic harm that has been inflicted upon me by the state and its beneficiaries. Yes, the government will build a few new homes. But not enough; nowhere near enough. Worst of all, the more hardworking and clean-living (and proud) poor people are, the less likely they are to qualify for subsidised state housing, and the more likely they are to be harmed by the Beds in Sheds crackdown. And – anyway – what right does the government have to define quality of housing, given the abominable conditions found on Britain's council estates? In the name of helping the poor, the state self-indulgently harms the poor.

8

The cost of free healthcare

If you think healthcare is expensive now, wait until you see what it costs when it's free.
– P. J. O'Rourke

We all know about the problems of the NHS. We've heard the horror stories. The pensioners left screaming in pain on trolleys in corridors. The surgeons operating on the wrong body parts, or leaving swabs sewn up inside wounds. The consultant whose manager told him to operate with a dessertspoon because the proper surgical tool was too expensive. The serial killer staff members whose activities go unreported by colleagues. The hospital-acquired infections (including deadly antibiotic-resistant bugs such as MRSA) that you are more likely to catch in an NHS hospital than in a private hospital in the UK. The harrowing story of Kane Gorny, the diabetic who died of thirst after nurses at St George's Hospital in London repeatedly denied him water; he called 999 from his own bed, to beg for help, but when the police came they were refused entrance to the hospital.

We've also heard the statistics that back up the stories of neglect, incompetence and inadequacy within the NHS. Stressed-out and overworked doctors are expected to see more and more patients in shorter and shorter consultations. Hundreds of hospitals have been closed over the last fifty years and not replaced, with the closures disguised as 'mergers'. The NHS now ranks poorly compared to other developed countries on key healthcare measures, including cancer survival rates, deaths from heart disease, stroke treatment, care of the elderly, lengthy waiting times, equipment availability, infant mortality, number of beds per person, and number of doctors per person. Recent decades have seen an increase in people fleeing to private healthcare, 'paying twice', i.e. once in taxes then again through insurance schemes or direct payments – although the NHS still accounts for around 83 per cent of health spending in Britain.

And the NHS has failed by its own standards. Since it was founded, health inequality in Britain has increased; the difference in life expectancy between rich and poor has grown.

"But the NHS is underfunded!" say the anti-capitalists. Not entirely true. Britain's expenditure on the NHS – annually around £110 billion, or roughly £1700 per head – is average compared to the healthcare spending of other developed nations, while, according to a recent OECD report, the NHS provides care which is 'poor to mediocre' compared to other developed nations. Moreover, when the New Labour government in Britain doubled spending on the NHS between 1997 and 2007, the difference in life expectancy between rich and poor accelerated. Something other than underfunding is hampering healthcare in Britain.

Here's another telling statistic: between 1999 and 2009, the number of managers employed by the NHS rose from 2.7 per cent to 3.6 per cent as a proportion of all staff. Following recent reforms, the figure today is 2.35 per cent, but in the last two years the number of managers has begun rising again. Currently, around half of the almost 1.4 million people employed by the NHS are not clinically trained (i.e. not doctors or nurses), while around 108,811 of the non-clinically trained employees are 'clerical and administrative staff' and 37,078 are 'managers and senior managers'. The top-heavy bureaucratic structure of the NHS is the result of a simple fact: outside of communist countries, the NHS is the most state-controlled health service in the world; indeed, it is the third largest state employer in the world, after the US and Chinese Armies. As we have already noted, if bureaucracy isn't checked by market forces then it has a tendency, in the long run, to bloat. Managers seek a bigger budget, while they and their employees prefer cushy office jobs to arduous or messy hands-on tasks. Whereas overly bureaucratic businesses go bust, the state doesn't; it grows more and more bureaucratic.

In 2001, Stuart Emslie, a civil servant, estimated that approximately £9 billion was wasted that year in the NHS. In 2011, the government announced that it was abandoning an attempt, started by New Labour, to create a single national database of patients' health records, £11.4 billion in total having been wasted on the failed scheme. Naturally, bureaucratic wastage indirectly compromises clinical care by sucking money away from patients. But the state also hampers clinical care directly within the NHS, in a multitude of ways.

First and foremost, bureaucracy hampers the work of doctors on the ground. In 2002, the Daily Telegraph published a letter from a consultant working in the

NHS who complained that his activities were being assessed – at national, hospital and university levels combined – by no fewer than 22 inspectorates. A similar article by another NHS consultant was published in the Daily Mail two years ago. The correspondent spoke of how he and his colleague friends 'are disillusioned, not with being doctors, or the practice of surgery, not with our colleagues or patients, but with an overwhelming sense that we have lost all power over our day-to-day professional lives'; he complained that NHS consultants are 'lost in a sea of bureaucracy over which they have little influence'. To comply with the state's ever-changing regulations, doctors must attend numerous meetings, read copious amounts of documentation, and complete huge amounts of paperwork. No doubt, some bureaucracy is inevitable within any organisation, but in the NHS the (fundamental) problem is that managers seldom wonder whether their interventions are helpful or not. Trained medical staff are, after all, highly capable and skilled individuals who, it is fair to presume, know better than bureaucrats how to carry out medical duties in a responsible way. Bureaucratic intrusions within the NHS often say more about managers trying to justify their salary, or maintain their influence, than improving the quality of care.

The doctor-writer Theodore Dalrymple has provided numerous insights into this strange and often darkly humorous world of NHS managerial mischief. In one essay, Dalrymple describes the experience of a consultant friend of his. The consultant, in preparation for his 'annual staff development review', was required to complete a lengthy 'personal development plan', and instructed to read a 19-page preparatory document (to help him 'get the most out of the meeting'), a document which in turn recommended the reading of six further documents, including the hospital trust's 24-page 'service plan' – all this despite the fact that he was a longstanding, trusted employee of the hospital. The meeting itself, as described by Dalrymple, was 'halfway between a police interrogation and a psychotherapy session'.

Other times, doctors are presented with lengthy questionnaires, which take hours to complete and feature patronising, obscure questions such as, 'In what way do you contribute to the quality of products?'. Indeed, Dalrymple contends, the very style of communication favoured by NHS bureaucrats hampers the work of doctors; obscurity wastes time and effort on the part of those who have to interpret it. For instance, in the 'service plan' that Dalrymple's consultant friend was asked to read there was a list of barely intelligible, abstract 'objectives', such as: 'Following production of the Strategic Direction Document, to make progress towards the production of a fully costed Strategic Outline Case (and ultimately full Business Case) which reflects "best practice" and addresses the requirements of the NHSE policy and guidelines'. Even the job titles of bureaucrats are confusing. Dalrymple recalls a manager whose position was '"Lead for NHS Productive Leader", a phrase so horrible it tortures the mind'.

When not infuriatingly obscure, the dictates of NHS bureaucrats are often downright irrelevant to the provision of healthcare. Receptionists of 45 years' experience are sent on mandatory 'telephone skills' courses. Twenty-two-page 'Dress Codes' are mailed to all employees. In one episode at Dalrymple's hospital, the management required all staff members to fill in a 'data cleanse' form, in which they were asked to specify their ethnicity, marital status, sexual orientation and religious affiliation. Never mind that this is an intrusion into the employees' privacy. Never mind that no list of categories, such as the 17 ethnicities defined on the form, could ever capture the true diversity of the hospital staff. And never mind the questionable purpose of the form: 'to help ensure that you continue to be paid correctly' (how can disclosing your race, sexuality, etc, be relevant to how you are paid?). The most sinister thing about the data cleanse is that it was a monstrous waste of time and money, in an organisation whose *raison d'être* is to provide healthcare to taxpayers. Obviously, no hospital should employ racist staff. But equally obviously, no hospital should spend other people's money on the moral grandiosity described by Dalrymple:

[...] the staff are about to be trained, yet again, on 'diversity issues'. Seven hundred of them are to be sent in batches of about 240 on three whole-day seminars on diversity to be held in a huge public arena [...] (lunch, teas and coffee provided, as well as free transport) [...]. For the hospital, the seminars represent at least three man years of labour, but that is only a small part of the cost. The arena is not cheap to hire, presumably, or the eight coaches needed twice on three different days. It is unlikely that the consultants hired to give the seminars are acting pro-bono [...].

Aside from its pointless expense, the impact of bureaucracy on NHS staff is similar to the impact of bureaucracy on teachers: it demoralises them. A recent report found that a 'mass exodus' of NHS staff is imminent because two thirds of them are considering quitting, citing reasons such as "overwork", "stress", the "restructuring/reorganisation" of the NHS, and "feeling undervalued due to managers' treatment of staff".

Bureaucracy also causes deviousness within the NHS workforce. To anyone who is ignorant of the history of collectivism, the periodic declaration of government healthcare 'targets' probably sounds wholesome, but, in reality, targets are a recipe for sharp practice. After politicians declared a four-hour target for admitting Accident and Emergency patients onto wards, it emerged that some hospital managers instructed ambulances to queue outside in the street, so as to prevent people from waiting longer than four hours inside the building. Another ploy was to redesignate hospital corridors as 'wards', and trolleys as 'beds'. Similarly, waiting times are a target ripe for manipulation by managers. One common trick is to offer patients a surgery appointment scheduled to take place within 24 hours of a consultation. When – more often than not – patients cannot attend at such short notice, they are thereafter excluded from the waiting times figures.

Sometimes targets lead to bare-faced deceit. A recent BBC survey found that one in twelve hospital managers admitted to submitting inaccurate reports to the government; the true proportion is probably higher. Bartholomew cites a manager who, upon supplying accurate figures, was dismayed to find himself warned by a senior bureaucrat: 'Do you realise if you submit these you'll be an outsider?' It is inevitable, notes

Bartholomew, that managers with integrity will, over time, be forced out of a system that applies pressure in this way.

More worrying still, a British Medical Association survey found that 60 per cent of doctors had firsthand experience of 'clinical priorities' being 'distorted' by 'politically motivated goals'. As Dalrymple puts it: 'doctors are paid not so much by result as by degree of conformity to directives.' When the American politician Sarah Palin opposed the nationalisation of healthcare in the US on the grounds that it would lead to 'death panels', that is, government committees that had the power to decide who would live or die, she was largely ridiculed and vilified in the liberal press. The (valid) point she was making was lost in the outcry: politicians should have no right to influence what clinical care an individual receives; the decision should be a matter for the doctor and his patient. (Or, if the patient's payment has been collectivised in some non-political way, for example through his membership of an insurance scheme, then the scheme's administrators might have a say by way of insisting that prior agreements about eligible treatments are upheld: but in this situation the individual payer still exerts an influence, having chosen which collective payment scheme to join in the first place.)

Bureaucratic rarefaction is instilled in the decision making of clinical staff right from the beginning, during their training. Before the NHS, doctors and nurses trained on the job, paying their way through contributing to patient care, but now they are trained by the state, for the state. It is no wonder that so many medical staff support the NHS vehemently despite their specific grievances within it. In recent years there has been a growing awareness that the training of nurses is overly academic. To achieve their professional status, nurses must complete a three-year degree course, during which, according to a retired nurse quoted by Bartholomew, they 'contribute virtually nothing to healthcare'. Worse, the academic nature of nurse training is probably putting off many people who would make good nurses. And worse still, the on-the-job attitude of nurses is subtly altered by their academic training. They are inclined less towards hands-on tasks and more towards box ticking. It is as if they are thinking, in the words of Bartholomew's source, 'I've got a degree. I am not going to get involved in giving personal care'.

The activities of medical staff within the NHS are also affected by the welfare ideology of anti-capitalism. By fostering generations of irresponsible miscreants, including drug takers, alcoholics, fat people and other self-destructive characters, the welfare state adds to the burden of healthcare in Britain – healthcare being just as much a 'right' as free money. To the detriment of responsible citizens, welfare miscreants receive NHS care no matter how irresponsible the behaviour that brought about their condition. To take one example among many: in 1950 there were no more than dozens of registered heroin addicts in Britain; in 2011–12 there were around 165,000, all of whom were enrolled in a free 'treatment programme', while 146,660 were given free prescriptions for methadone, a 'replacement' drug that many addicts either take in conjunction with heroin or sell on the streets. Of course, none of this is really free: it is paid for by people who don't take heroin. (Incidentally, much of the public sympathy directed at heroin addicts is based on falsehoods. As Dalrymple has argued at length in *Romancing Opiates*, withdrawal from heroin is not purgatory: it is no worse than having a cold. And heroin addicts are not passive victims of their social milieu: if they were, then how come the majority of people from that same milieu choose not to take heroin?)

Not only do Britain's welfare miscreants waste time and money in the NHS, they, too, exert a distorting effect on doctors' clinical judgements. Many doctors admit to flippantly prescribing pills or other NHS services so as to fob off, as quickly as possible, truculent patients whose only real problem is their freely chosen lifestyle. Many doctors also confess to writing sick notes under duress from patients. Dalrymple quotes how a doctor friend of his justified doing so: 'the last patient whom I made fit to work when he didn't want to return to work picked up my computer and threw it at me. We ended up having a fight on the floor.'

The NHS has become so notoriously dysfunctional its financial resources have increasingly been turned towards improving its reputation in the eyes of the public. Government bodies whose ostensible role is to regulate or administer the provision of healthcare – the National Institute for Clinical Excellence, NHS Improvement, the Care Quality Commission – today have expensive 'communications' offices, as do individual hospitals. Unlike in the private sector, in the NHS the extent of marketing is not linked to previous or prospective returns; indeed, since we've already paid (via our taxes) for the services of the NHS, it is unclear what returns its marketers are expecting at all, other than career advancement for themselves and their bosses. Dalrymple recalls an episode in which his hospital erected huge banners displaying 'Nine Promises' to the public. Presumably, 'wasting money on indulgent PR stunts' was not among the promises.

And yet people still believe in the promises of the NHS; it is a revered institution in Britain. There is a taboo against even considering alternative ways to deliver healthcare; any politician who denounced the NHS would thereby commit electoral suicide. As a result, the history of healthcare in Britain is almost unknown. People assume that before the NHS only the rich had access to medical services. Let's again turn to James Bartholomew to see how inaccurate this belief is.

Healthcare was of course patchy in medieval times, which was no bad thing: in those days, doctors were so ignorant of science they usually made patients worse. By the nineteenth century and beyond, however, medicine had come on in leaps and bounds. This was especially true in Britain, where medics played a major role in arguably the five most important advances of the era. The development of vaccines, anaesthesia, antiseptics, antibiotics, and an understanding of how to prevent cholera, all took place in Britain before the NHS.

And, yes, Britain had hospitals. At the beginning of the twentieth century there were around 600 of them. Over half of the 64 hospitals in London today were founded in the nineteenth century. One of the most respected, St Barts, was founded as far back as the twelfth century. Though some pre-NHS hospitals were built by local authorities, most were charities, set up by philanthropic individuals, community organisations, doctors or religious groups.

In keeping with the variety of hospitals available at the time, there was no uniformity in how or how much people paid for treatment. The most indigent patients were treated for free. Others were assessed by an Almoner as to their ability to pay and were charged accordingly. Others paid via their Friendly Society membership, and many hospitals themselves ran insurance schemes similar to those of the Friendly Societies. After 1911, some hospital care was funded by National Insurance.

Similarly, there was diversity within hospital staff with respect to their remuneration. The highest-ranking individuals – consultants – gave much of their time for free. They saw this as their duty, having learned their trade within the system as students. Consulting was an opportunity both to continue learning and to pass on that learning to new students. The role also came with an enormous amount of prestige. Nurses, too, sometimes worked for free. For many, the role was a vocation; they lived, ate and worked in hospital quarters. Some nurses were nuns.

Doctors who ran general practices were also paid in a variety of ways. It has been estimated that in the early twentieth century 20 per cent of people were treated for free by GPs, who typically adjusted their fees according to the ability of people to pay. Other times GPs negotiated fees with Friendly Societies or workplace insurance schemes, or ran insurance schemes of their own, or were paid via National Insurance. Some Friendly Societies had in-house doctors. Some GP surgeries were 'provident dispensaries', which were funded by benevolent individuals but also charged patients a small fee.

Healthcare before the NHS was characterised, in

other words, largely by competition and charity, both of which are forces for good. Charity brought out the best in its givers and receivers, while competition improved doctors and hospitals, and drove costs down for patients. Both charity and competition fostered a can-do, entrepreneurial spirit among healthcare providers, who were always seeking to attract either funding or custom, especially the custom of the various health insurance schemes, including those of the Friendly Societies. Any doctor who ripped people off didn't last long; this, combined with charity, kept healthcare within the reach of the poor; 'the vast majority of the poor were treated', as Bartholomew sumarises.

The instillation of market discipline also kept hospitals efficient and clean; wasteful, dirty institutions put off patients. In contrast to the layers of management crammed within hospital walls today, pre-NHS hospitals were run by small teams. Dr Maurice Slevin, from the Centre for Policy Studies, has noted that some consultants 'are old enough to remember the days when a large teaching hospital was run by a governor, a matron, an accountant and several secretaries'. The matron, of course, is a figure who has been enshrined in legend: with her fearsome mop and frown, *she* above all ensured that the hospital was kept clean and orderly.

But in 1945 a change was about to take place that would sweep all this away. When the Labour Party won power after the Second World War, its MPs sang 'The Red Flag' – the anthem of socialism – on their first day in the House of Commons. A few years later Britain experienced 'the most radical state take-over of healthcare anywhere outside an avowedly communist country', as Bartholomew puts it. The blueprint for a 'National Service for Health' had been sketched out in 1943, in a Labour Party pamphlet with that title, written by Michael Young. In 1946, Minister of Health Aneurin Bevan pushed through health reforms based on the recommendations of the pamphlet. In 1948, the NHS was launched.

This much of history is well known. Less remarked upon is *why* the Labour Party thought that a National Service for Health was needed. You will probably be as astonished as I was to discover that in Young's pamphlet there are hardly any criticisms of pre-NHS healthcare. There simply wasn't much to criticise. Instead, the pamphlet emphasises how 'unplanned' the available healthcare was, with its 'medley' of institutions. In other words, bureaucratic state control combined with nonchalance about real results was built into the NHS right from the start.

That's why doctors at the time repeatedly voted against Bevan's proposal. They understood that the NHS would compromise their independence and the care available in Britain. One doctor declared that the state was proposing the 'biggest appropriation of property since the dissolution of the monasteries'. So how did Bevan persuade doctors in the end to concede? 'I stuffed their mouths with gold', is how he put it. Doctors went where the money was. Unnecessary expenditure was built into the NHS right from the start.

With members of the public being forced to fund the NHS, and with doctors receiving higher pay in the NHS than elsewhere, the plethora of freely chosen, nongovernmental health insurance schemes inevitably withered away; most of their members couldn't afford to pay for state healthcare *and* private health insurance, and the private schemes couldn't afford the fees the state was paying the doctors. On the eve of the foundation of the NHS, Bevan described Tories as 'worse than vermin'. However, despite his and his colleagues' rhetoric of egalitarianism, in reality the NHS took power from the working classes and gave it to the professional classes.

And the process is ongoing. Notably, it accelerated when New Labour invested heavily in the NHS at the turn of the millennium: GPs' salaries simultaneously underwent a sudden inflation. In his superb book, *Life After the State*, Dominic Frisby quotes 'an anonymous NHS trust chairman' who describes the deal that doctors enjoy within the NHS today:

[...] GPs are, bar a handful, self-employed. Each practice is a small business. Through the British Medical Association (BMA) they block-negotiate with the government and it's a totally closed shop. The contract GPs have is endless, as in it is theirs forever. No, not for life – forever. When they wish to retire they hand that contract to someone of their choice, if they are qualified. It is a guaranteed income forever. The contract also guarantees them rent on a building they buy – nice earner. The NHS also supplies their computers and IT support. How many other businesses get a deal like that? By working the system GPs can earn huge sums and do as few hours as they wish. And the GPs with the worst health outcomes always seem to be the ones making the most money. Consultant clinicians and those in acute care have similarly ridiculous contracts. Look on the halo above the head of doctors that work in the NHS with extreme scepticism. This has been going on since the NHS was founded.

Frisby sums up the situation nicely: 'doctors now enjoy privileges beyond even the loathed, titled aristocracy of yesteryear. A simple dynamic is missing: the NHS is run to suit its suppliers; it should be run to suit its customers.'

"But what about America and Cuba?!" cry the anti-capitalists, referring to the allegedly unfair (and allegedly entirely private) healthcare system in the US, and the allegedly brilliant healthcare available in communist Cuba.

As for the latter, it is largely a myth. Up until the dissolution of the USSR, the Cuban government plunged large Soviet subsidies into hospitals, thus artificially raising the quality of healthcare in Cuba relative to countries of comparable poverty (poverty, note, which in Cuba was caused by communism). In keeping with the nature of state-run services, there was (and still is) a large amount of corruption and deceit within Cuban healthcare – patients jumping queues by giving 'gifts' to administrators, infant deaths in childbirth not being recorded – yet, for a while, you could indeed get an appendectomy in Cuba if not a pair of shoes. But in recent decades the service has deteriorated. Last year, an international SOS health survey cited Cuba as a 'high risk' travel destination, a place where getting ill is dangerous.

Similarly, there are many myths about US healthcare. Anti-capitalists are always expressing outrage at the fact that some people in the US do not have health insurance. But, when you peer beneath the surface, the truth about the (approximately) 12 per cent of US citizens without health cover is far from being morally clear-cut. At the time of writing, disabled citizens and the poorest people in the US have health cover, by way of the government scheme Medicaid which funds the treatment of those who cannot work or cannot afford health insurance. And *all* US citizens of more than five years' standing are eligible for healthcare assistance from 65 years or older, by way of the government Medicare scheme. The 12 per cent, in contrast, are neither poor enough nor disabled enough to qualify for Medicaid, nor old enough to qualify for Medicare. In effect, the anti-capitalists who wring their hands about the plight of the 12 per cent are bemoaning the fact that the Americans who paid into health insurance funds do not pay for the treatment of people who could have paid into similar funds but chose not to. I'd like to see how anti-capitalists would react if, say, their own workplace salaries were mandatorily shared with employees who voluntarily never turned up to work.

Another criticism of healthcare in the US is that it is callously expensive because private companies fleece the public. It is true that healthcare in the US is expensive. The world-leading quality of US medical provision comes at a world-leading cost – indeed, value for money in US healthcare is among the lowest in the world. But this is largely because healthcare in the US is not private enough. The government is the biggest health insurer in the US, and pays for over half of all healthcare spending. A large part of this spending involves giving lucrative contracts or subsidies to medical companies, in effect giving them monopoly control over certain sectors of healthcare, meaning that those companies are able to charge captive patients excessively. Another reason for the expense of US healthcare is that so little of it is paid for out of pocket. Patients usually pass on their medical bills to an insurer – whether a government or private insurer – confident in the knowledge that the other members of the scheme will pick up, on average, 85 per cent of the tab. As a result, individuals do not shop around much, and the medical companies have less of an incentive to drive prices down. It doesn't help, of course, that most US insurance schemes are huge and impersonal; in such schemes – of which government schemes are the most pronounced examples – patients feel scant obligation to their fellow insurees.

For all its problems, healthcare in the US is far less government-controlled than in neighbouring country Canada. And – lo and behold – the quality of healthcare is higher, and health inequality is lower, in the US than in Canada. Tellingly, the filmmaker Michael Moore created a 'documentary' pillorying the US healthcare system and praising socialised medicine, yet when Moore sought treatment for being too fat, he went to a clinic in Florida. Not Canada, or Britain, or Cuba.

The world over, healthcare systems benefit from at least some element of market competition. Under socialism, the more work hospitals do, the less money they keep; in a market system, hospitals profit the more work they do, leading to more and better healthcare provision. Under socialism, there are few incentives for keeping healthcare bureaucracy under control, quite the opposite; in a market system, hospitals are incentivised to be efficient. Under socialism, there are scant rewards for innovation in health; under a market system, innovation pays. Under socialism, bureaucrats decide what healthcare you receive; under a market system, you decide, or at the very least you choose your insurer. Under socialism, there are longer waiting lists and lower consequences for medical malpractice; under a market system, people are treated more promptly and more safely. Under socialism, access to healthcare (like access to education) is determined by your level of political influence and your intelligence – the NHS is 'egalitarian in theory only, not in practice', as Bartholomew puts it; in a market system, doctors provide treatment at prices more people can afford. Under socialism, people have less of an incentive to behave responsibly with respect to their health than under a market system.

Under a market system, a dog that injures its leg can get a scan the very next day. Under socialism, humans wait and wait and wait for medical treatment. As John Stossel concludes: 'Healthcare is too important *not* to be disciplined by market competition.'

9

Top-down, down, down

Yes, in socialism, the rich will be poorer – but the poor will also be poorer.

– Thomas Peterffy

Anti-capitalists firmly believe that when bungling governments try to manage society from above this can cause great harm to a country and its people – so long as that country has recently been invaded by a Western power.

In 2003, the US began its 'shock and awe' military campaign in Iraq. Within weeks, dictator Saddam Hussein's regime had been defeated, and a puppet government had been installed. At this point, a new bombardment began – of US dollars. It is estimated that, to date, $60 billion has been spent on 'reconstruction' efforts following the war in Iraq.

Across the political spectrum, commentators agree that American attempts at 'nation building' in Iraq have been incompetent and corrupt. In 2004, nearly four hundred tonnes of shrink-wrapped US dollars were loaded onto military aircraft and transported to the region. But what happened next no one really knows. Much of the money spent in Iraq has simply melted away. The US government pressurised officials into quickly handing out cash to companies that were supposed to rebuild national infrastructure – but much of the work was never done. Funds were allocated to firms who sketched proposals on the proverbial back of a cigarette packet. American company Custer Battles was given $15 million to provide security at Bagdad airport, including sniffer dogs at checkpoints. Colonel Richard Ballard recalls that the company turned up with *one* dog: 'He would be brought to the check-point, and he would lie down. And he would refuse to sniff the vehicles [...] I think it was a guy with his pet, to be honest.' $900,000 was awarded to a building firm that was supposed to build a farmer's market – the result being a few concrete slabs and a tin roof. And millions more were spent on gimmicky 'Hearts and Minds' projects – such as handing out croissants – through which US soldiers sought in vain to appease the bombed, maimed and displaced Iraqi population.

Worst of all, officials often simply stole reconstruction money by writing cheques for fake employees. Corruption was all too easy: the task of auditing post-war spending in Iraq was entrusted to a consulting firm that was operating out of a private home in San Diego.

These various snapshots have been described by John Stossel in *No They Can't*. Stossel also notes that much the same incompetence and corruption occurred after the war against the Taliban in Afghanistan, where a US Special Inspector General has reported that $55 billion of reconstruction money remains unaccounted for. At one point, a UN agency was given $150 million to rebuild an Afghan village destroyed by the US military. The UN took a 20 per cent cut and hired a contractor. He took a cut, and hired another contractor, who likewise took a cut, and so on. In the end, the subcontractor who carried out the work only had enough money left to pay for some wooden beams. But it was the wrong type of wood, so the locals used the beams as fuel. This was 'the ultimate illustration of the futility of the government's efforts', rues Stossel – '$150 million up in smoke'.

Every anti-capitalist knows that no colonial government has ever achieved anything more than questionable results in the course of intervening in its conquered nation's economic affairs. Yet, strangely, anti-capitalists fail to draw the correct general conclusion, i.e. that the economic planning of rulers tends to be woefully inadequate when it comes to fulfilling the needs of millions of citizens. The best decisions come from free people, who are more motivated to improve their lives than a government supposedly acting on their behalf. And whereas free people can adjust quickly when things go wrong – leading to innovation and progress – government planners adjust slowly, if at all. The government workers who have the largest incentive to respond to feedback are (elected) politicians, but the temporally distant threat of being unelected hardly compares to the real-time incentives faced by free people trying to succeed for themselves. Meanwhile, government bureaucrats have a large incentive to lie to their bosses about the results of the politicians' policies; no one gets promoted for reporting failure to a senior bureaucrat. When you add in the fact that all government workers are tempted to keep public money for themselves rather than spend it on the public, or at the very least to spend it profligately so as to demonstrate to the budget-holders that the money was 'needed' and will be needed again, the prospect of enlightened government planning recedes into negligibility.

Indeed, even if every bureaucrat had the best will in the world, the social-engineering tasks that governments set themselves are far too huge and complex to be planned and carried out successfully by mere mortals.

In healthcare, welfare, housing and education, and many other sectors of the economy, government bureaucrats forcibly corral resources that would be better deployed by free people in a free market, or by free people acting charitably. The term 'regulation' is a mantra of anti-capitalists, and it symbolises their urge to rule and control people. Of course, we need some rules in society. But in the hands of anti-capitalists, regulation becomes a stick with which to beat capitalists, and this punitive form of regulation tends to backfire and hurt poor people above all.

Consider how regulation works. Businesses are made to pay rates to the government, so that planners can create and uphold various rules within a particular sector. Often, businesses are made to prove in advance that they'll stick to the rules; this proof comes by way of various licenses and qualifications that companies or employees must acquire before they start trading. So who do you think defines these rules and the licensing criteria? And who is most affected by regulation? Governments, naturally, consult with established businesses when setting the rules, meaning that those businesses are minimally inconvenienced by the rules, and may even benefit from them, or at the very least benefit from providing the consultancy service. Meanwhile, newcomers are hit hardest by the rules. Newcomers struggle to afford the rates that must be paid to the government so as to ensure the rules can be enforced. Newcomers can't afford to pay corporate lawyers to navigate the rules. Regulation has the side effect of keeping newcomers poor. As Stossel puts it, 'government intervention – licenses, taxes, regulations – makes it harder to go from being a "little guy" to owning the means of production'.

With this in mind, government regulation should be kept to an absolute minimum, so as to protect consumers and workers where necessary while harming small businesses as little as possible. Much of the burden for 'regulation' of businesses can be borne by insurance companies. Insurers impose sensible rules – rules designed to prevent businesses from being negligent towards their assets, workers or customers, or other people's assets (thus saving the insurers money in repair bills or lawsuits), while also ensuring that businesses can continue to make a profit (thus allowing the insurers to continue to get paid).

Alas, the extent of the red tape in which Britons today are embroiled indicates the preeminence of anti-capitalists. In modern Britain, you are required to possess a government license or qualification to rent out more than two rooms in your house, play music in a theatre production, run a massage parlour, deal in scrap metal, run a minibus service, open boarding kennels, run a hairdressing salon (in some areas), run a childminding business, be a teacher (in most state schools), run a pet shop, work as an art therapist, and engage in many, many other kinds of activities (although, admittedly, the situation is rosier in Britain than in some US states where you need a license to be a *florist*). Year in year out, the regulations governing various sectors of the economy grow more and more voluminous. This is partly because, constitutionally, laws are more easily created than redacted. But a further cause of the accumulation of rules is the insatiable megalomania that motivates anti-capitalists in government.

Even when there is a superficial reasonableness to government interventions that aim to strip power from the wealthy, those interventions often backfire. We have already seen that 'rent controls' designed to protect the poor against 'exploitative' landlords simply deter house builders, leading to housing shortages, which harm the poor above all. The minimum wage, much vaunted by anti-capitalists, has a similar effect on job creation. Companies that can't afford to pay the minimum wage simply can't hire staff, meaning that more people remain unemployed; the poor suffer. And, of course, smaller companies are affected most by the higher wage costs imposed by the minimum wage, so the minimum wage hurts the little guy whether he is an employer or an employee. Indeed, when governments propose a minimum wage they usually receive the support of big businesses, who know that their competitors will be crushed by higher costs. Support also comes, typically, from the Unions, even when their members already receive more than the minimum wage; they know that it is in their interests to force competitors out of the market.

Another way in which governments attempt to subdue capitalists is by introducing stricter employment laws designed to protect people in their jobs. But the harder it is to fire people, the less likely businesses are to employ people. The unemployed – the poor – benefit from laxer employment laws. Much the same logic impugns laws that ban companies from offering internships. Working for free sounds like exploitation, until you take into account the fact that interns get free training, job experience, and a foot in the door. Banning internships closes doors on the unemployed.

Even health and safety laws can do more harm than good. Labyrinthine government regulations can discourage companies from being attentive and innovative when it comes to protecting employees or customers; safety can become a distracting bureaucratic box-ticking exercise with no relevance to reality. At the other extreme, unregulated businesses are not as hazardous and incompetent as people assume. Stossel's book features a fascinating graph showing that workplace fatalities in the US were in decline long before 1971 when the federal government's Occupational Health and Safety Administration was founded. It's not just the strictures of insurers but the motives of free people that help keep businesses conscientious. Businesses don't want their employees or their customers dead, employees don't want to die at work, and customers don't want to be harmed by businesses; these forces drive safety standards upwards, aided by the burgeoning wealth and technology that capitalism affords us. 'Government is like someone who gets in front of a parade and pretends to lead it', declares Stossel.

Governments today are particularly fond of trying to prevent employers from mistreating members of 'discriminated against' groups, such as women, older people, ethnic or religious minorities, homosexuals, and disabled people. Anti-discrimination laws provide recourse for employees to take legal action if they are dismissed, underpaid, overlooked for promotion, or subjected to various workplace disadvantages. This sounds enlightened, but anyone acquainted with human nature can see that these laws run the risk of simply reducing levels of recruitment from the protected groups. Employers may reckon that they are less likely to be sued one day by an employee who doesn't have special protection than by an employee who does, or employers may simply shy away from the level of regulation they'll have to deal with if they employ someone who has special protection. In this way, anti-discrimination laws may surreptitiously harm the very people they are seeking to protect.

Alas, that's what happened in the US when the Americans with Disabilities Act was passed in 1992. With its slew of complex regulations, the ADA requires businesses to make 'reasonable accommodation' for disabled employees, and to provide 'easy access' for disabled customers. No doubt, these laws have helped some disabled people. However, according to an MIT study, the Act was followed by a decline in employment among disabled men aged 21–58, and among disabled women aged 21–39. In his book *Disabling America*, disabled author Greg Perry has lambasted the ADA, poignantly declaring that he is glad he grew up before it came into existence.

Behind many anti-discrimination laws there is a lack of appreciation for capitalism. After all, it's not as though businesses left to their own devices are hothouses of discrimination – quite the opposite. Businesses only exist if they make money, and money cannot discriminate. As Milton Friedman puts it: 'The great virtue of a free market system is that it does not care what colour people are; it does not care what their religion is; it only cares whether they can produce something you want to buy.' Knowing this, businesses are motivated to ensure that their premises, products and services are as congenial as possible to as many customers and employees as possible; shutting down opportunities for mutual gain is commercial suicide. Furthermore, businesses can deliberately aim to serve groups that have specific needs. Both within and between societies, capitalism has been driving tolerance forward for centuries; anti-capitalists sit in the passenger seat and claim the credit while barking off-putting instructions.

Capitalism also embodies a form of inclusivity that ought to delight anti-capitalists (but doesn't). A free market fosters a complex division of labour and therefore creates meaningful – indeed, indispensible – economic roles for people who are not especially talented or capable. In capitalism, almost anyone can play their part, and be rewarded for it, as attested to by the improved living conditions of poor people across the generations. Of course, there will always be some citizens who are so incapacitated they are unable to contribute productively. There is no question that they ought to be supported, the only question being whether the state or a more localised system of welfare is best equipped to do so. But, in either case, the wealth generated by capitalism is essential to providing that support; undermining businesses through anti-capitalistic regulation is in no one's interest.

Meanwhile, when combined with welfare policies, anti-discrimination laws can have the effect of intensifying the risk of dependency among members of the protected social groups. Giving people free money while also telling them that they deserve the money because society systematically discriminates against them is a double whammy of apathy inducement. In the US, anti-discrimination policies combined with welfare have led to housing projects where black residents seethe with hopeless resentment. In Europe, the same can be said of the impact of welfare policies combined with the rhetoric of 'Islamophobia' on young Muslims.

Again and again, anti-capitalism backfires in its attempts to help people on the margins of society. This dynamic can be seen, fundamentally, in anti-capitalism's harmful obsession with equality. Yes, by generating wealth, capitalism generates inequality, just as a fun party generates noise. But, in absolute as opposed to relative terms, poor people are made less poor by capitalism; capitalism affords poor people better houses, health, life expectancy, jobs and bank balances. Businesses, at the end of the day, make money from the poor by benefitting the poor. In contrast, anti-capitalists, supposedly on behalf of the poor, control the resources of society via the government in such a way as to make poor people absolutely poorer – while also, on the whole, making them less educated, less healthy, less motivated, less responsible, less family-oriented, less moral, and less likely to get a job.

Perhaps worst of all, anti-capitalism renders all members of society less inclined towards engaging in genuine acts of kindness and community-spiritedness. When almost half of the wealth of a country is forcibly seized by government workers who squander it on disastrous policies and grotesque levels of bureaucracy, when genuine workers toil for increasingly long hours to pay increasingly heavy taxes to public sector bureaucrats who are increasingly vehement in their rhetoric of improving society on everyone else's behalf, most people lose the will and the wherewithal to contribute to society by other means. Social capital and charity decline in proportion to socialism's appropriation of the wealth of capitalism. Even our very *aspirations* towards kindness, benevolence and dutifulness fade out when government action is allegedly the worthiest exemplar of such qualities. And when people make less of an effort to help each other, the neediest are hit hardest.

In fostering financial and spiritual poverty, anti-capitalists ensure that they themselves, despite their rhetoric of egalitarianism, retain their wealth and security relative to most members of society. In the end, anti-capitalists condemn the West's actions in Iraq and Afghanistan for precisely the wrong reason. They fail to understand the difference between economic globalisation and top-down, impositional governance. Economic globalisation is generally a good thing: it lifts countries and people out of poverty; it gives people jobs. Even a third-world child who works long hours in a sweatshop is better off than if she had no job at all, or if, in desperation, she was forced to work as a prostitute (an all too common eventuality). In contrast, top-down, impositional governance leads to corruption and failure every time. Anti-capitalists fail to understand the difference because in the West they are the executors and sole beneficiaries of top-down governance, and their *raison-d'être* is to disrupt capitalism. Anti-capitalists are scapegoaters. The capitalistic West is their scapegoat, even though, overseas and at home, it is Western government workers, not businesses, that wreak most havoc. Capitalism gets the blame for the sins of its bureaucratic blamers, and the blamers share the spoils amongst themselves.

Meanwhile, capitalism becomes a caricature of itself.

10

Scapitalism

We often forgive those that have injured us, but we can never pardon those that we have injured.
— François de La Rochefoucauld

When, in 2013, David Cameron gave a speech referring to 'self-satisfied socialists', it was easy to dismiss his remark as yet another example of the rough-and-tumble of politics. But there was a deep wisdom in Cameron's epithet. Socialists – anti-capitalists – generally *are* self-satisfied, in the dictionary sense of deriving satisfaction from their own activities and in their own judgments. Certainly, anti-capitalists can take no pride in the tangible effects of their ideology – unless, of course, the results sought were government corruption and waste, and an increase in poverty, stupidity, immorality, crime, and ill health.

The self-satisfaction enjoyed by anti-capitalists arises from their scapegoating of 'capitalists', i.e. of businesspeople and economically liberal voters and politicians. Through blaming capitalists for the disastrous impact of anti-capitalist governance, anti-capitalists enjoy similar psychological payoffs as were enjoyed by scapegoaters in centuries past. Anti-capitalists enjoy sadistically watching capitalists squirm. They enjoy having a clear (or, perhaps I should say, cleared) conscience; someone else is guilty, never they. They enjoy the deluded comfort of knowing that the horrible aspects of life – suffering, poverty, meanness – are not arbitrary and meaningless, are not inevitable, but are the outcome of the supposed malevolence of capitalism. They enjoy the (spurious) sense of togetherness afforded by their ideology: we, the group, the society, the good guys, stand together against the lone hawks of capitalism. They enjoy a release from rumination: capitalists are nasty and there's an end on't. They enjoy the purity of their viewpoint: lucre is filthy, socialism is untainted. They enjoy the luxury of avoiding making a realistic, practical and cooperative effort – whether through participating in business, trade or a local community – to improve society. And, above all, they enjoy not being scapegoated themselves: there is safety as well as solace amid the crowd.

And then of course there are the rewards that accrue to government-employed anti-capitalists, of whom in Britain there are several million, the executors of the bogus good intentions of anti-capitalists among the electorate. Government workers earn more money than their counterparts in the private sector (on average, £5000 more), essentially because the taxpayer, not the management, picks up the tab. Government workers are the beneficiaries of generous pension packages (and often private healthcare). Their job security is higher; it takes *a lot* to get sacked from the public sector. (When I worked for Brent Council briefly, after completing my PhD, one of my colleagues sat at her desk all day playing the card game 'patience' on her computer; no one objected.) Public sector bureaucrats have easy jobs even at the worst of times. Who wouldn't prefer lounging in an air-conditioned office, drinking coffee and whimsically composing a strategy report, over, say, abseiling down the side of an oil rig? Yet public sector workers are granted longer paid holidays, enjoy more flexible working hours, work shorter hours, and take more leave through 'sickness' than their counterparts in the private sector (on average 17.5 days compared to 7.2 days, respectively, according to the Work Foundation).

The witchfinders of centuries past benefitted handsomely from scapegoating. Their ruse was simple: identify some source of naturally occurring discord or bad luck, enter the fray, use demotic rhetoric to inflame people's scapegoating tendency and thus further distract them from the reality of the situation, consolidate accusations against the chosen scape-goat(s) through spiralling legal interventions, and – in sum – profit from making the situation much, much worse. Similarly, today, anti-capitalists within the government benefit handsomely from scapegoating. Their ruse is alarmingly familiar: identify a source of naturally occurring discord or bad luck (in this case, associated with the problems of poverty, uneducated children, immorality, crime, and ill health), enter the fray, use demotic rhetoric to inflame people's scape-goating tendency and thus further distract them from the reality of the situation, consolidate accusations against the chosen scapegoat(s) (in this case, capitalists) through spiralling bureaucratic regulations, and – in sum – profit from making the situation much, much worse.

Common to the witchfinders and their duped communities, and the government anti-capitalists and their misguided supporters within the electorate, is a collective commitment to scapegoating and its rewards. All the individuals involved in modern scapegoating relish the opportunity to relieve themselves of their own guilty sins, of their own contribution to the social and economic disaster wrought by anti-capitalism. Just as the ancients cast their sins onto wretched scapegoats who sat in chains in the market-place, anti-capitalists cast their sins onto scapegoated capitalists.

No doubt, anti-capitalists will respond – with their lips curled in indignation – that it is absurd to compare rich, greedy capitalists with poor, pathetic scapegoats. But the comparison is apt, when you consider the economy as a whole. Scapegoats, recall, are often selected for their strength, for their ability to bear the burden of others' sins; scapegoaters sap the strength of their scapegoats in much the same way that misbehaving teenagers sap the patience and energy of their parents. Accordingly, capitalism is chosen as a scapegoat by anti-capitalists precisely because it is strong – and, indeed, because anti-capitalists are envious of capitalists. The result is an economy that, as a whole, displays strength *and* weakness. Some businesses remain strong enough to endure or even thrive amid the onslaught of bureaucratic demonisation, while others – smaller and weaker businesses – succumb. It is notable that anti-capitalists often speak wistfully of 'small businesses', as though big businesses are the real enemy. Don't be fooled by the rhetoric. Anti-capitalism's straightjacketing regulations are responsible for strangling small businesses. The practice of immersing the economy in suffocating taxation and red tape, then lamenting the passing of small businesses, is analogous to the practice of 'swimming' witches; in the eyes of the anti-capitalists, any business that succumbs is innocent, whereas any that survives and thrives is guilty.

It is true, of course, that capitalism is powered by 'creative destruction' – that is, by unproductive businesses dying and productive businesses thriving and thereby capitalism causes inequality, but there is an intuitive fairness involved – in principle – in the growth of a business that attracts customers, and in the death of a business that doesn't. To earn money is – usually – to perform a favour and receive the promise of reciprocation; to accept payment from a customer is to receive an 'I owe you'. Some businesses don't earn many IOUs, and go bust; other businesses earn lots of IOUs, and their owners grow powerful, in the sense that they can exchange those IOUs for other people's favours. It is hardly fair – or practically desirable – to lament this kind of earned wealth.

As IOUs have proliferated throughout the modern world, providing more opportunities for IOUs to be transferred from person to person – i.e. the more that capital, and capitalism, has spread – the potential customer base for people with good ideas has grown. In turn, some businesses have become increasingly rich compared to others. Products or services that are particularly helpful – that do a lot of people a big favour – can today more than ever attract a huge influx of IOUs. The writer Nassim Taleb describes our modern world as 'Extremistan'. Linked into a global economy, we can now readily perform favours for millions or even billions of strangers through our work. This panoramic economic landscape features extreme levels of prosperity and mutual understanding, and extreme levels of inequality. But, insofar as people earn their wealth through performing favours, Extremistan is worth cherishing. The broom of capitalism gets dirty, but it sweeps away poverty and war.

Despite the protestations of anti-capitalists, the only way to reduce inequality is to *increase* competition. This means not swamping the little guy with taxes and regulations. If he comes up with a good new method that is more beneficial to people than the rich guy's method, or if he comes up with a method that helps people in some new way, then his idea, like a green shoot, needs to be left to grow, not swamped. Nor should the little guy be drip-fed money that has been forcibly expropriated from the big guy. Welfare dependency inspires no green shoots at all, leading to entrenched inequality. Similarly, our modern so-called 'Nanny State', which attempts to control more and more of our lives 'for our own good', has a subduing effect on people's sense of get-up-and-go. The more you limit people's choices, the less people take responsibility for their lives.

And the more you try to replace social capital with top-down social engineering, the more you hamper the development of the open-minded spirit that is required for making a contribution to the economy – a deficit which weakens the poor especially. Local communities are often caricatured as hubs of insularity and xenophobia – an evaluation that is undoubtedly sometimes true – but it is also true that communities comprise the only means of instilling in citizens a willingness to engage co-operatively with strangers. In other words, xenophobia in human beings is a default setting, which can be amplified or eradicated depending on the mores of a community. By fostering social breakdown among the poor, anti-capitalist welfare policies leave some people psychologically stranded in a default mindset of xenophobia, a mindset which makes them less likely to get ahead by trading and partnering with members of wider society and beyond. Social capital, as Robert Putnam observes, tends to make communities richer; conversely, a lack of social capital tends to make communities poorer.

As for anti-capitalists, they, too, are left psychologically stranded by their lack of social capital. Granted, anti-capitalists congregate socially, and when they do so, they behave warmly towards one another. But it seems to me that these gatherings involve a lot of backslapping and parroting of *bien pensant* views and not a lot of genuine mutual support and concern – in other words, not a lot of social capital, the constructive, collaborative, realistic, practical community-spiritedness that brings so many benefits to its participants as well as to wider society. Similarly, anti-capitalists in their government workplaces do not so much support each other as monitor each other's toeing of the line.

Relatedly, it also seems to me that anti-capitalists are prone to accumulating problems (self-inflicted or otherwise), the reason being, perhaps, that scapegoating inhibits scapegoaters from addressing their own problems and from caring about each other's problems. Interestingly, studies suggest that conservatives tend to be happier than liberals; perhaps conservatives are more mutually supportive than liberals, and therefore have more of a genuine sense of belonging. Another interesting finding is that anti-capitalists are more likely than conservatives to indulge in drinking or drug-taking. Assuming that these activities are largely indulged in socially, the predilection of anti-capitalists towards narcosis aptly symbolises their preference for a phoney kind of social capital. Members of a scapegoating group don't do each other much good through their mutual association, and nor do people who get drunk or take drugs together. Metaphorically – and, many times, literally – socialist social capital is narcotic social capital.

No wonder anti-capitalists have so much 'sympathy' for welfare miscreants, whose state-sponsored chaotic lives of indulgence arguably mirror the lives of so many anti-capitalists. And no wonder the default xenophobia found among some poor people mirrors the lack of genuine openness typically displayed by anti-capitalists. Openness to strangers means, after all, openness to trade; you're not really, truly open to someone unless you're willing to work with them towards mutual gain. Devoid of the genuine social capital through which a mindset of openness is cultivated – and lacking the clear-headed realism that this openness is based on – anti-capitalists contribute very little to modern economic life, and a lot to authoritarian governance, which appeals naturally to people who are afraid of their fellow men. In this respect, the only difference between xenophobic anti-capitalists and xenophobic poor people is that anti-capitalists are sly enough to hide their real beliefs behind the ramparts of political correctness.

By swamping society in regulations, and by generating apathy and xenophobia among sections of the poor, anti-capitalism turns the economy into a caricature of itself. A society's naturally occurring level of inequality – a level which is already high in our hyper-connected modern world, where big fish swim in a big pond – is exacerbated by government interventions that deflate would-be entrepreneurs and undermine social capital. In other words, anti-capitalism indirectly makes economically powerful people more powerful by keeping the poorest people poor.

Anti-capitalism also makes powerful people more powerful by changing their behaviour directly. Insofar as scapegoating weakens the scapegoat, it also makes him tougher; the more unloved he is, the coarser he becomes. Today, the hardened temperament of the scapegoat is exemplified – among other ways – in the rich guy's fight to stay rich. It is important for all of us to keep money aside for a rainy day, but in an economy swamped by taxes and regulations, where falling to the bottom is doubly perilous, the rich guy hoards his wealth. Moreover, when taxes are spent corruptly and damagingly, the rich guy is more likely to make use of tax-avoidance schemes, or commit outright tax fraud. (This is one of the reasons, as John F. Kennedy observed, that lower taxes can lead to higher tax revenues.) And when the rich guy can't get decent NHS healthcare for himself or his family, or a decent state education for his kids, he covets money even more tenaciously. The hoarding imperative induced by anti-capitalism is psychological as well as economic. The incivility caused by anti-capitalism – in particular, by educational failure and welfarism – makes everyone's lives more stressful. In an anxious, anti-social atmosphere, the rich guy – literally and figuratively – builds a taller fence around his house and installs bigger bars on his windows.

Worse still, in a society that is depleted of social capital, in a society that is dominated by a growing cohort of anti-capitalists who downplay or denounce civic engagement, the rich guy has fewer opportunities to express himself in community-spirited ways. Faced with millions of people who are psychologically stunted by the effects of anti-capitalist governance – people who find meaning through emulating uncouth celebrities rather than contributing to a community – the rich guy discovers that 'conspicuous consumption', not charity, is often the best way to attract esteem. Instead of bankrolling a group meal, or sponsoring the village fete, or paying for a new wing of the local hospital – instead of displaying 'conspicuous charity' – he buys a flashy watch, a newer car, or a bigger mansion. We all want esteem. When engaging with communities, we seek it in pro-social ways; when engaging with a society atomised by anti-capitalism, we seek esteem in socially divisive ways.

Of course, not all rich people are show-offs – far from it. As Putnam has observed in his latest book, *Our Kids*, rich people are more likely, not less, to cultivate social capital of a genuine and open kind, and this tendency further consolidates their economic power. Conservatism is often sneered at for its popularity among 'Little Englanders', among groups such as the Women's Institute, The Masons, and so on. But the sneering is simply anti-capitalist propaganda in disguise. Little Englanders produce and consume social capital at the weekends, and trade open-heartedly with the world during the week.

Another of the ways in which the pressure of anti-capitalism consolidates economic power is by prompting businesses, not just rich individuals, to grab and hoard resources. No doubt, the level of financial risk involved in running a business should never be underestimated; therefore some level of prudence is necessary and understandable in commerce. But caution can shade into cupidity. Shady commercial practices such as tax avoidance and gaming the system, for instance, become more tempting the higher – and therefore the closer and more threatening – the waterline of tax and regulation.

Yet, simultaneously, in an economy dominated by anti-capitalism, businesses also have opportunities to collude with governments; there is a fine line between regulation and collusion, as we saw in the previous chapter. In the USSR, 'licensed traders' were seen as a legitimate means of bringing about revolutionary ends. Similarly, the government today uses businesses to fulfil its aims. There are many types of public-private arrangements. Some businesses sell goods or services to the government. Other businesses provide or manage services, e.g. hospitals, schools and trains, on behalf of the government; these so-called public-private partnerships ballooned in numbers under New Labour at the turn of the millennium. Still other businesses provide goods or services to the government but are partly funded by taxpayers – public-private organisations. Finally, some businesses part-fund government initiatives, e.g. when a supermarket rents a retail unit in a social housing block.

Public-private arrangements reward companies that agree to submit to government influence. Such arrangements exacerbate the top-heaviness of the economy. The bigger a business is, the more useful – the more powerful a tool – it is to bureaucrats, so big businesses enjoy a head start over their rivals when it comes to winning government contracts. And the perks often continue long after the tendering process.

The government can draw on unrivalled funds in the areas in which it acts, meaning that its business partners can crush competitors.

Sometimes, bureaucrats award a business an exclusive legal right to perform a particular function; in that situation, a business takes on the monopolistic powers of the government, and can therefore charge extortionate prices. A good (i.e. bad) example is the company that carries out criminal record checks on people who want to work with children. To work with children you have to apply for a certificate that confirms your suitability based on your criminal history. To obtain this certificate, you must pay £44 to a company called the Disclosure and Barring Service. Even children are not permitted to work with other children without being vetted; between 2002 and 2009, 43,000 under-16s and 3000 under-13s had DBS checks. Moreover, if you move into a new role that also involves working with children, you have to apply to the DBS all over again, that is, even though you already have a DBS certificate, and presumably you had good references from the first position. It all makes for a nice little earner for the DBS. Government contracts are a gravy train for a few lucky companies. (Furthermore, it is reasonable to wonder whether, by creating expense and suspicion, the imposition of criminal checks on people who want to work with children has a destructive effect on social capital.)

Another problem with public-private arrangements is that they encourage an unproductive form of competition between businesses. On the open market, businesses mainly compete to be the most cooperative, that is, they compete in terms of how much they succeed in establishing mutual gains (between themselves and customers, and between themselves and other businesses). So, under capitalism, the process of competing is productive for almost all the businesses involved, as well as all their customers, which is all of us. But, under the influence of anti-capitalism, businesses seek cosy government contracts, and therefore compete with each other by way of a tendering process from which taxpayers, and most of the businesses involved, earn nothing. When anti-capitalists bemoan the 'competitiveness' of modern economic life, they mislead.

Indeed, the tendering process is not just unproductive, it is expensive and wasteful. The bureaucratic hoops that the government makes its prospective business partners jump through are held out by lots of salaried bureaucrats. There are also jobs for bureaucrats once the process is complete; consultants and other hangers-on spring up liberally amid public-private arrangements. Set upon both by bureaucrats and businesses, the hard-earned money of taxpayers is like a carcass at the centre of one of those swirling, aquatic feeding frenzies you see in wildlife documentaries. You often hear free-market supporters describe public-private arrangements as 'the worst of both worlds'. Hitherto-scapegoated companies relish the competitive opportunity to engorge themselves on public money and power the instant they win the favour of the government, yet they do so whilst operating with the limited effectiveness enforced by the bureaucratic straightjacket of anti-capitalism.

The area where, above all, we could do with a little more competition – genuine, capitalistic competition – is the housing sector. Over the last 15 years in Britain, more than £23 billion of government money has been awarded to 'housing associations'. These public-private organisations build social housing on behalf of the government, but tend to build at a more sluggish rate than commercial builders. The bureaucrats and the housing associations, not to mention private homeowners, are all benefitting from a system of restricted supply enforced by government regulation. Less regulation and more competition in the housing sector would drive prices down, for buyers and renters.

Like poisonous gas, collusion between governments and businesses is deadliest when its presence isn't obvious. Such was the case in the run-up to the Great Recession of 2008. To fund precipitous levels of spending, the New Labour government oversaw a huge housing bubble. Banks were encouraged to lend money to low-income buyers who were ill-equipped to afford the mortgage repayments. The new buyers, combined with the housing shortage, fuelled a surge in house prices, which boosted government tax revenues. But, of course, no bubble lasts. When the low-income buyers defaulted on their mortgages, panicked savers caused a run on Northern Rock, an episode that sent shockwaves through the UK economy, and pushed other banks to the brink. In response, the government used public money to bail out the stricken banks, thus protecting the bankers who had hitherto enabled the government to sustain its spending. This last part is crucial. Most commentators blame the banking crisis on 'deregulation' – as though the bankers bore sole responsibility for the crisis because the government had supposedly opted out of responsibility. But, surely, the government knew exactly what was happening. Holding back the supply of housing while the banks lent money irresponsibly was part of an overall regulatory strategy for extracting money from taxpayers. The first part of that strategy was to maintain and strengthen the predatory housing regulations that, over generations, had led to the formation of a housing bubble, and the second part was to sanction the inflating of the bubble by the bankers. Taxpayers paid, and are continuing to pay, for the whole fiasco, while bankers and their cronies in the government have been paid handsomely throughout. And, as usual, the poor have suffered the most, led astray by the easy credit made available to them by the bankers and politicians.

High taxes are another inducement to collusion between businesses and governments. When rich companies stand to lose a lot of money through taxation, they are more tempted to bribe bureaucrats or politicians, who may provide tax loopholes for a small fee. Other kinds of shady financial deals between governments and businesses include import restrictions and loan guarantees, as well as subsidies and bail-outs. All of this chicanery makes for a complicated tax system, which leads to more hassle and expense for everyone. It also leads to puppet politicians. And it leads, once again, to rich businesses stealing a march on poorer rivals.

Across the political spectrum, commentators are increasingly aware of the problem of collusion between bureaucrats and big businesses. The apt phrase 'crony capitalism' is often used to describe our economic system, dominated as it is by cosy relationships between big businesses and the state. But anti-capitalists draw exactly the wrong conclusion – that we need more regulation, more bureaucrats, more government control, more straightjacketing of the economy, more businesses engorging themselves on taxpayers money, more opportunities for corruption. The right conclusion is spelled out by Stossel: 'There is a smarter way to get corporate money out of politics: shrink the state. If government has fewer favours to sell, citizens will spend less money trying to win them.' If the carcass of taxpayers' money is smaller, fewer hungry feeders will congregate around it.

Under anti-capitalist governance, under the pressure of scapegoating, businesses behave like orphaned street kids who fight for every privilege. Although big businesses are arguably the worst offenders, the coarseness of scapegoated capitalism is reflected throughout the economy. Whatever its stature, a scapegoated business is less likely to treat its staff well, pay its staff well, train an apprentice, employ a disadvantaged person out of reasons of decency or loyalty rather than productivity, market its products honestly and without manipulation, strive for quality not superficial appeal, charge an honest price, eschew profiteering, decline to make money from legal but ethically dubious products and services (e.g. alcohol, tobacco or gambling), provide a friendly 'human' service to customers, support local charities through sponsorship or donations, respect the environment, and patronise local artists.

And, of course, a major contributor to all these shortcomings is a lack of social capital. When businesses lose their embeddedness in a community – and are answerable primarily to distant shareholders or bureaucrats – they lose some of their sense of responsibility, some of their humanity. For example, in days gone by, pub landlords refused to serve drunks, because drunkenness was considered shameful in the eyes of local communities. Now, faceless chains of theme bars offer sales promotions that are deliberately designed to squeeze every last penny out of intoxicated, insensible revellers.

You hear a lot from anti-capitalists about businesses today being 'exploitative'. This is largely an inaccurate term, because no business forces its customers to buy its products or services. But the term also contains a germ of truth. Monopolistic state-supported businesses take advantage – for instance, through higher prices – of the fact that customers have nowhere else to take their custom. And all businesses behave more coarsely the more intensely they are scapegoated. In desperation, some scapegoated businesses take advantage of the system, or seek to hoodwink customers into making purchases that aren't necessarily in those people's interests. Crafty accountants, clever lawyers, pushy salespeople, shameless marketers; all these are largely symptoms of the rise of anti-capitalism, of scapegoated capitalism.

The coarseness of scapegoated capitalism – of 'scapitalism', to coin a word – also affects individuals up and down the economic ladder. It is not just the rich who become more avaricious and sly amid a flood of taxes and regulations. And the general mood of bonhomie is hardly lifted by the moral nihilism induced in poor people by the state's failures within welfare, education and health.

The anti-capitalists are correct that our modern economy is, in many ways, a harsh, mean, grossly unequal, corrupt, manipulative and inhospitable arena. When they bang on about 'decency', they have a point; in our modern society, people are less civic-minded, considerate, open hearted, thoughtful, self-controlled, and charitable than generations past. But anti-capitalists have no right to complain about the status quo, and no right to insist on their favoured form of redress. Anti-capitalist governance relentlessly exacerbates the shortcomings it claims to alleviate. It exacerbates them through disastrous interventions in education, housing, health and welfare, and through swamping the economy with regulations. And it leads to bureaucrats and politicians colluding with big businesses in such a way as to make those businesses more monopolistic and powerful. Above all, anti-capitalism contributes to the moral deterioration of capitalism by scapegoating all businesses and businesspeople, causing them to become harsher and less conscientious the more they are blamed for the failings of the anti-capitalists. In other words, the harder the capitalists fight for their survival, amid the toxic atmosphere of anti-capitalism, the more the anti-capitalists are motivated to protest. The grip of anti-capitalism is snake-like; struggling against it makes the grip tighten. And – to extend the metaphor – the more the snake feeds on its prey, the bigger it grows.

11

Scapegoatalitarianism

Evil originates not in the absence of guilt; but in our effort to escape it.

– Shannon L. Alder

A couple of years ago, Republican nominee Mitt Romney stood against incumbent US Democratic President Barack Obama in a two horse race for the White House. Most commentators agree on the exact moment Romney's horse stumbled, never to catch up. At a fundraising event, Romney was filmed remarking, off the cuff, that '47 per cent of Americans pay no taxes. So our message of low taxes doesn't connect... There are 47 per cent of the people who will vote for the President no matter what'.

The public outcry was instant and devastating. Pundits on the left accused Romney of not caring about the whole US population, while many Republicans accused him of the strategic crime of *seeming* not to care about the whole population. With much of the media frothing with indignation – no doubt aiming to appeal to (or provoke) an indignant audience – Romney himself was forced into a humiliating (and pusillanimous) climbdown, claiming that his comments didn't 'come out right'. Very few people defended him.

But what exactly had he done wrong? Whether or not the precise figure was correct, the point Romney was making was not unreasonable. People who work for the government don't technically pay taxes; they are paid by taxes. And people who receive welfare don't pay taxes; they are supported by taxes. Naturally, government employees and dependents are highly likely to vote for any political party – such as the Democrat Party – that advocates tax-and-spend policies. With good justification, Romney believed that these policies tend to be bad for the rest of the population – and, ultimately, bad for most of the 47 per cent too. The suggestion that he was displaying contempt towards the electorate was breathtaking in its hypocrisy. The suggestion was, of course, based on scapegoating. The instant he dared to point out the truth, the 47 per cent along with their friends in the media projected *their* contempt for the electorate onto Mitt Romney the scapegoat.

How has it come to this? How has a nation whose constitution enshrines 'life, liberty and the pursuit of happiness' become mired in stultifying bureaucracy, paternalistic regulation and the dismal pursuit of government authority? How has a similar growth in taxation and cack-handed state power occurred in Britain? Will the West soon reach a tipping point, whereby the electoral constituency of capitalism is no longer large enough to halt the spread of anti-capitalism throughout government and society? And what will happen when that tipping point is reached?

Like all forms of scapegoating by groups, anti-capitalism is a tragedy of the commons. A tragedy of the commons occurs in any situation where individual members of a group seek advantages over their peers in such a way that when all members of the group follow suit there are collective disadvantages for all the group members – disadvantages that outweigh the advantages accruing to individuals. Like black holes, tragedies of the commons drag in increasing numbers of bystanders. Any group member who doesn't participate in a tragedy once it is set in motion, who doesn't seek the advantages available to him as an individual, faces the prospect of a double whammy: losing out as an individual and suffering the same collective disadvantages as the rest of the group.

The psychological benefits of anti-capitalism, and the material benefits enjoyed by anti-capitalists in governance, come at the expense of wider economic and social decline. At this moment in time, the tragedy of anti-capitalism is in motion, dynamic, expanding; it is gathering momentum and participants. There will come a time – maybe that time has already come – when the harms inflicted by anti-capitalists on wider society are so deleterious to all of us that those harms outweigh the advantages which anti-capitalists currently enjoy as individuals.

The momentum of a tragedy of the commons is also perpetuated by the tendency of its participants to deceive themselves about their role and its consequences. Self-deception is a sure-fire way for people to avoid the double whammy – personal losses and collective harms – suffered by anyone who declines to participate in a tragedy. Instead of facing up to those prospective losses and actual harms, participants in a tragedy turn a blind eye; they deny that their behaviour is either selfish or collectively harmful. In other words, participants in a tragedy deceive themselves about the reality of their situation – about the reality of their guilt, and the reality of the world around them – precisely because they know they are guilty and they know of the collective harms to which they are contributing.

Similarly, anti-capitalists deceive themselves about having benefitted from harming wider society. They can see with their own eyes that, over the course of half a century, their efforts within education have resulted in delinquency, illiteracy and despondency; their efforts to rehabilitate and house needy people have resulted, largely, in metastasising irresponsibility, incivility, unemployment, drug addiction, and family breakdown; their efforts to provide universal free healthcare have resulted in health inequality and shoddy treatment combined with relentlessly expanding costs borne disproportionately by the poor; their efforts to regulate the economy have resulted in increased unemployment, discrimination and inequality, while destroying small businesses and making big businesses more powerful; their efforts to pin the blame on capitalism have resulted in a harsher, less benevolent economy wherein scapegoated businesses fight coarsely for their financial lives; their efforts at social engineering have undermined social capital and led to all the devastating consequences that inevitably follow from a dearth of community life; while their efforts to aggrandise themselves and increase their own bank balances have been resoundingly successful. Anti-capitalists can see all this, which is precisely why they deny it to themselves and blame capitalism. Their outer knowledge of their destructiveness, combined with their inner knowledge of their guilt, is too much for them to bear – both prospectively and retrospectively. Sometimes it is easier to lie to oneself, and select a scapegoat, than to admit prior responsibility and make amends.

That's why talking politics with an anti-capitalist can be such a frustrating experience. Just as you can't reason with an alcoholic, you can't reason with an anti-capitalist. The more carefully and rigorously you point out the flaws in anti-capitalism, the more irrationally and vindictively an anti-capitalist will respond. Refusing to engage with the subject matter and abusing his interlocutor are the only ways that an anti-capitalist can deflect attention away from the truth when it is pointed out to him. Upon hearing the truth – which he knows very well to be true, deep down, in the part of himself about which he is deceived – he instantly recognises the pitfalls, the shame, of his assenting. So he changes the subject, mangles his logic, misrepresents what is being claimed, blusters with outrage, and attacks his interlocutor. Ann Coulter summarises:

> If you can somehow force a liberal into a point-counterpoint argument, his retorts will bear no relation to what you've said – unless you were in fact talking about your looks, your age, your weight, your personal obsessions, or whether you are a fascist. In the famous liberal two-step, they leap from one idiotic point to the next, so you can never nail them. It's like arguing with someone with Attention Deficit Disorder.

Actually, it's like arguing with someone whose subconscious attention is resolutely trained on the truth and on their guilt, while their conscious attention is strategically shattered, its sharp edges strategically wielded.

In the face of an onslaught of determined, incoherent vitriol, combined with the psychological and economic attractions of joining the massed ranks of anti-capitalists, it is no wonder that over the last half-century the British population has been increasingly lured, electorally and economically, by anti-capitalism. If you can't beat them, join them: this is especially true when beating them in a logical argument ensures that you lose by other means, and joining them brings additional payoffs.

To a large degree, the rise of anti-capitalism has consisted in an increasing number of people diving into a black hole of tragic self-deception. But another – and arguably more damaging – contributor to the slow death of capitalism has been the Judas-like pusillanimity of successive Conservative governments. Public spending (adjusted for inflation) rose gradually under Margaret Thatcher then carried on rising under John Major, and the current Conservative administration has done little more than even out the precipitous rise that occurred after New Labour came to power in 1997. The profligacy of recent Conservative governments, combined with Tony Blair's reputation as an alleged capitalist, has been a boon to anti-capitalists, because, in the eyes of the electorate, social and economic breakdown has come to be blamed inaccurately on 'capitalism' rather than accurately on soaring public spending and backfiring bureaucracy. A Conservative government that betrays its capitalistic principles by pandering to anti-capitalism is like a surgeon who tries to promote the efficacy of his work by deliberating botching the job yet pretending that he did his best. I can think of no better analogy for the way in which the current Conservative administration is, bizarrely, describing its fiscal policy as 'austerity': there has been a decrease *in the rate of increase* of public debt, but an increased debt overall.

Yet it is also tempting to be sympathetic to the present government. Former Tory policy adviser Steve Hilton, who worked alongside David Cameron in Downing Street, has spoken of his dismay at the relentless power of the unelected bureaucratic machine in Britain. Bureaucrats regularly announce expensive policies while the government fundamentally disagrees and is powerless to intervene. 'The bureaucracy masters the politicians', says Hilton. In the US, the late Ronald Reagan expressed similar frustration about how he failed during his presidency to reign in the public sector and curtail public spending.

Increasingly, bureaucracy is mastering public sector workers, too. An Audit Commission survey found that, when public sector employees quit, the reason they cite most commonly is 'bureaucracy and paperwork'. It is surely not (entirely) true that bureaucracy is increasing because bureaucrats don't like bureaucracy, so most of the quitters must be employees, including frontline staff, who value the achievement of practical results and who dislike being hampered in their jobs. In effect, anti-capitalist bureaucrats are squeezing proactive and conscientious 'proper' workers out of the public sector. The bureaucracy of anti-capitalism accumulates in society like limescale in a kettle.

"But what about Scandinavian countries?!" shout the anti-capitalists, in a final, rearguard action. "Norway, Sweden, Finland, Denmark, Iceland: they are great places to live, but they have higher levels of taxation and public spending than most countries, including Britain!"

The part about higher taxation and higher public spending is true. But the Scandinavian countries, far from being utopias, face many of the same problems as us, or worse. All the Scandinavian countries are more unequal than Britain, as measured by the percentage of wealth owned by the wealthiest 10 per cent of citizens. All the Scandinavian countries are among the twenty most expensive places to live in the world, with Norway, Iceland and Denmark being more expensive than Britain. All but Iceland and Norway have a higher level of unemployment than Britain. All but Finland have a higher level of average household debt than Britain, with Denmark's figure being the highest in the developed world. All have a higher suicide rate than Britain. All but Finland have a lower-ranking education system than Britain. Overall, the picture in Scandinavia is much the same as in Britain: statism is a liability. Sweden has some 250,000 pensioners living below the EU poverty line, and is riven by racial tension. Iceland has not yet fully recovered from a near-total economic collapse in 2008. Norway is stuttering as its oil dries up and the far right now has the support of almost one in six people. Denmark's poverty levels have doubled in the last twenty years. Finland has been stuck in recession for four years, with some 250,000 people unemployed and one of the highest murder rates in Western Europe.

Tellingly, Scandinavian countries tend to do better than Britain insofar as they are *less* statist than us, not more. For instance, all provide better healthcare than Britain – but none has a health system that is nationalised to the extent of the NHS. And Scandinavian countries are notorious for their social capital, despite their high levels of government spending. Perhaps, in the harsh climes and scattered settlements of Scandinavia, community life is more evidently a necessity; notably, the Danes have a much-cherished tradition of cultivating 'hygge', a word for which there is no English translation, but which roughly means 'cosy, communal togetherness'. Because of their abundance of social capital, Scandinavian countries enjoy a high level of political decentralisation, which perhaps helps mitigate some of the negative effects of high government spending. In turn, decentralisation and high social capital combine to form the high levels of trust found in Scandinavia. Arguably, it is the Scandinavians' characteristic agreeableness, not their taxation model, that endears their countries to the world.

One final comparison is particularly noteworthy. A quarter of a century ago, Sweden permitted some schools to opt out of the state education system. These 'Free Schools' were the inspiration behind Gove's education reforms in Britain – although, in Sweden, more radically, all parents were given 'vouchers' and permitted to choose their children's school. Free Schools comprise around 14 per cent of all Swedish schools but have proven popular and successful. Their introduction saw an upturn in Sweden's international ratings in education, but this was followed by a recent downturn. In response, politicians on the left in Sweden have vociferously blamed Free Schools for the national decline in educational standards. It's an argument with a depressingly familiar logic: the failings of the 86 per cent of Swedish schools that are still run by the state are being blamed on the 14 per cent of schools that are thriving outside of the state.

Meanwhile, in Britain, unchecked by our moribund levels of social capital and by pusillanimous Conservatives, the limescale of anti-capitalist, statist bureaucracy continues to accumulate. Around half of the British population is now carrying the other half, while the carriers are subjected to the resentment of those they carry. Public discourse has become increasingly fractious, with more and more people pointing the finger of blame at anyone with a load on his back. The US conservative writer John Hawkins has remarked on the darkness that lurks at the heart of anti-capitalism:

As a political philosophy, liberalism is centered around hatred and divisiveness. Liberals don't promote their ideas so much as they try to turn people against those who get in the way of their ideas. Liberals lie to minorities and tell them that conservatives hate them, they tell women that men hate them, they tell the poor they should hate the rich. They try to pit the successful against the unsuccessful, the workers against the corporations – and they regularly talk about their own country like it is one of the most godawful places on earth. That means liberals are, at best, extraordinarily cynical people who're willing to manipulate people for political gain – and at worst, it means that they believe all this nonsense.

Actually, self-deception makes both alternatives true. Anti-capitalists consciously believe in their philosophy of hate precisely because they know, subconsciously, of the harms it causes and the gains it shamefully brings them.

Those of us who consciously reject the logic of anti-capitalism ought to be worried. Hatred can lead to violence, via many paths. For instance, violence promises to soothe the anger of its perpetrators; a festering sense of injustice can spur people into taking the law into their own hands. Similarly, ideology is a powerful inducement to violence. In the mind of an ideologue the prospect of a radically fairer world – where billions of people live in prosperous harmony – justifies any intervention, no matter how extreme. Both of these motivations tempt anti-capitalists to resort to violence, as does the logic of scapegoating. Anxious to prove their commitment to the cause, in large part so as to avoid being scapegoated themselves, today's anti-capitalists are increasingly exhibitionistic. In a climate of phoney moral one-upmanship, violence offers a potential means of flaunting one's virtue. There is a fine line between a permanent scapegoat and a dead scapegoat.

We should be particularly worried about the proliferation of hatred within our government. For good (Hobbesian) reasons, governments possess a monopoly on the use of force when it comes to resolving disputes within the populace. But when anti-capitalists in government get to define, based on a calculus of hatred, who has wronged whom, state power can mutate into an invincible weapon against scapegoats. Throughout history, bungling governments have always practised scapegoating, but in a healthy democracy – one with an impartial legal system, a sophisticated media and a discerning electorate – political incompetence can't hide forever behind untruth. In contrast, when the apparatus of government is swollen and inflamed by anti-capitalism, when the electorate, the law and the media have, as a result, been badgered, cajoled or battered into sympathy, the government can escalate scapegoating with impunity.

The paradigmatic example of this is communist Russia. After the 1917 Revolution, anti-capitalists killed some fifty million of their fellow countrymen. Some were executed for political dissent; some were murdered simply for being rich; some died in the labour camps through which the regime attempted, futilely, to manage the economy; others died of starvation, the government having destroyed the only economic system, capitalism, which is capable of feeding a nation. The revolutionaries were supposedly implementing a perfect system of governance, so – to save face – their failures had to be blamed on someone else. But, of course, failure under communism is always unyielding, so the government was unyielding in its scapegoating. Supposedly, there were enemies at large within the populace; the Bourgeoisie, like witches, were sworn 'Enemies of the People'. There were enemies beyond Russia, too – evil imperialist forces forever sabotaging the efforts of the communists. And there were enemies plotting within the government itself; Stalin's 'show trials' culminated in the execution of thousands of people, including officers of the regime.

Anxious not to be the next victim of the government's persecutions, Russian citizens eagerly reported each other to the authorities. Even staying quiet was considered suspicious. Family members, friends, colleagues – all sent each other to the Gulag. As Anthony Daniels explains in *The Wilder Shores of Marx*: 'If you are held responsible for what I do and I am held responsible for what you do, does that make us not friends but mutual spies? Normal human bonds are dissolved by collective responsibility, to be replaced by distrust, fear, dissembling and withdrawal.' Just as medieval witch trials tore communities apart, communism, beginning with its precursor, anti-capitalism, turns people into mutual enemies, locked into an arms race of phony righteousness.

Throughout history, every time a country's government has been overrun by communists, the same story – of economic failure, blame, murder and paranoia – has played out. In Maoist China millions died of starvation, while middle class citizens were dragged from their homes then beaten to death by gangs of ideological youths, egged on by the state. In communist Cambodia, under Pol Pot, the policy of forced collectivisation led to the deaths – through famine or state murder – of millions. In communist Romania, Albania, Vietnam, North Korea and Cuba, more of the same, to varying degrees of brutality.

Even Nazi Germany, usually thought of – inaccurately – as a right wing phenomenon, followed a similar path. As Dan Hannan has pointed out, Hitler considered himself a socialist – a National Socialist. He admitted that 'the whole of National Socialism' was 'based on Marx', the difference being that Nazis were 'doers' not 'pen pushers'. (And it is well known that Hitler held great appeal among Anglophone left wing intellectuals, such as George Bernard Shaw, H. G. Wells and Jack London.) Of course, most of the scapegoats chosen by the National Socialists were Jews, but this itself demonstrates a further continuity between Nazism and socialism. Jews were the most productive members of German society; they were bankers, powerful businessmen, civic leaders. So strong was the resentment the Jews inspired in their fellow Germans it led, ultimately, to systematic government violence, and a nation sunk in collectivist failure. (Today, anti-Semitism still crops up regularly within socialism: Israel is the bogeyman of the left. As Theodore Dalrymple has pointed out, 'if anti-Semitism is the socialism of fools, socialism is the anti-Semitism of intellectuals'.)

A scapegoatalitarian state is one in which collectivists dominate the government and systematically blame and violently attack the most productive members of society, namely, the capitalists. In all such cases, the population's descent into barbarism takes the form of a tragedy of the commons, a tragedy that continues until it implodes under the weight of its own collective harms. The historian Hans Mommsen has argued that the Nazi state consisted of a jumble of rival bureaucracies that sought power through displaying and exercising ever-increasing anti-Semitism, that is, through an arms race of moral exhibitionism that led ultimately to the Holocaust. Revolutionary Russia was characterised similarly by a ferment of socialist factions vying for power and influence over a disaffected populace. Once in motion, the German and Russian scapegoatalitarian tragedies – like so many others – proved impossible to halt. The level of intensity and absurdity reached by such tragedies is symbolised by a story told by Solzhenitsyn, and recounted by Jonathan Glover in *Humanity*:

At the end of a Party conference in Moscow Province, a tribute to Stalin was called for. Everyone stood and clapped wildly, for three minutes, then four, then five. The clapping became more painful. It was a kind of physical embodiment of the trap people were in. Who would dare be the first to stop? The Secretary did not dare, as his predecessor had been arrested, and the NKVD [secret police] men were there watching. The painful applause went on past ten minutes, with everyone trapped in it. Among those on the platform was the director of a paper factory. After eleven minutes of applause, he sat down, followed by everyone else. That night, he was arrested. He was given ten years on some pretext, but his interrogator told him never to be the first to stop applauding.

As this example hints, in a scapegoatalitarian society the presence of a tyrannical leader is as much a symptom as a cause of collectivism. An authoritarian leader provides a much-needed source of social coordination in a society whose members have renounced normal human bonds. At the heart of anti-capitalism is little more than a void, amply demonstrated by what becomes of a society when it kills its capitalist scapegoats. Like those oceanic feeding frenzies that dissipate into fragments and emptiness, all the sound and fury of anti-capitalism, with its blustering moral grandstanding, its frenzy of bureaucratic destruction, its temporary nourishment of bureaucrats, and – when all this concludes, as is all too likely, in scapegoatalitarianism – its violence, leaves behind next to nothing.

For as long as I can remember, I have been fascinated by the question of why a society would allow itself to sink into state-led barbarism. Surely, I thought, individuals would see that they were contributing to a situation that was morally wrong, and take evasive action. I didn't reckon with the momentum of a tragedy of the commons combined with the power of self-deception. In a tragedy of the commons, individuals do the wrong thing, in the sense that they contribute to a collective disaster so as to avoid missing out on moderate selfish gains. In self-deception, individuals know they are doing the wrong thing and therefore they rigorously deny it to themselves – they passionately tell themselves that they are doing the right thing – so as to ensure that they can continue to reap the temporary rewards of selfishness. Therein lies the answer to my question. A society descends into scapegoatalitarianism whenever its members, en masse, seek collectively destructive advantages over one other, while deceiving themselves into fervently believing that their cause is noble. When people groupishly and self-deceptively insist on the avoidance of evil, they bring about evil. Deep down, they know they're in the wrong, which is why they *don't* take evasive action.

The (otherwise appalling) film *The Educatorz* nicely illustrates this mindset. The film is about a trio of German anti-capitalists who regularly break into the houses of rich people, where they create a big mess and leave behind sinister graffitied messages (e.g. 'your days of plenty are over'). The self-styled 'Educatorz' are oblivious to the human cost of their antics, until they break into the house of a middle-aged businessman who arrives home and catches them in the act. They kidnap him at gunpoint and take him to his holiday cottage in the mountains, where they plot their next move. Gradually, however, the man begins to befriend them. He explains to them that when he was younger he was a dope-smoking 'idealist' just like them; they are cautiously impressed. He reminisces about how he started a family and took a steady job and gradually lost his old activism – but he still believes in their cause, albeit not their use of violence. The kidnappers suddenly see (half of) the light. They admit that kidnapping him was wrong. But they still think that breaking into his house was morally acceptable – and so does he, apparently. The film ends with the man giving them permission to live in his mansion, to use it as a base from which the Educatorz can continue their campaign of burglary and disruption.

What is notable and troubling about the film's denouement is that the Educatorz display no understanding of the high probability that their anti-capitalist activities would sooner or later have led to violence, and would likely do so again. The trio allow themselves to believe that it is acceptable for them to carry on their campaigning, precisely because they know where it will lead and they know that facing up to this fact will bring them shame. They have learned something about the nastiness at the heart of their ideology; so they lie to themselves so as to learn nothing consciously. This allows them to continue indulging in their righteous activities unperturbed, while also enjoying a nice warm house, lots of bottles of beer, cigarettes, and many more of the accoutrements of capitalism.

Anti-capitalism, with its tragic logic and self-deception, has ensconced itself in the home of democracy, with the permission of a huge swathe of the British electorate. As yet, making a scapegoat of capitalism has ushered in a weaker, coarser, more contemptible economy but hasn't led to state violence. Among the anti-capitalists there are still plenty, it seems, who realise, on some level, that a permanent scapegoat is more useful alive than dead. Nonetheless, we are undoubtedly witnessing communism's 'long march through the institutions', as per the famous rallying cry of the German socialist Rudi Dutschke. Whether or not that march will end in bloodshed will depend in large part on the ability and willingness of capitalists (genuine capitalists, as opposed to those who are feeding from the government trough) to bear the burden and retain their democratic influence.

I don't hold out much hope for persuading anti-capitalists to abandon their marching. The power of tragic self-deception is too strong. And so is the fear of nature, of strangers, of uncertainty, that makes scape-goating so alluring in the first place.

12

The weather machine

All over the world, strangers talk only about the weather; all over the world, it's the same, it's the same.

– Tom Waits, 'Strange Weather'

'Humanity stands at a defining moment in history. We are confronted with a perpetuation of disparities between and within nations, a worsening of poverty, hunger, ill-health and illiteracy, and the continuing deterioration of our ecosystems on which we depend for our well-being.' Up until the last clause, you'd be forgiven for assuming that this excerpt came from the Communist Manifesto. In fact, it came from 'Agenda 21', a UN environmental 'Action Plan' to which 179 countries signed up in 1992, with further (increasingly binding and restrictive) regulatory commitments agreed in 1997, 2002, 2012 and 2015. Marx's dream of a communist world government didn't catch on universally in the twentieth century, but it's catching on now. The modern emphasis on the 'continuing deterioration of our ecosystems' is making all the difference.

Of course, not all environmentalists are anti-capitalists, and vice versa. But there is a significant overlap between the political agendas of 'Reds' and

'Greens'. Most environmentalists are anti-capitalists and most anti-capitalists are environmentalists – 'redgreens', as it were. In what follows, it is these redgreen environmentalists whom I have in mind. As we will see, the alliance of environmentalism and anti-capitalism has been a boon to both causes, helping bureaucrats benevolently destroy economies and societies the world over. Strangers are decreasingly trading with each other and increasingly talking only about the weather – and, above all, about what governments can do about the weather. Somehow, environmentalism is speaking loudly and urgently to the part of human nature that hankers after state control, whether to exercise it or submit to it. How come?

To be fair, environmentalism surely stems in part from a genuine and laudable desire among people to conserve the natural world, for themselves or their children. Generally speaking, despoiling the environment is like fouling your own nest – an obviously bad idea – and, equally intuitively, the natural world has some measure of intrinsic value. But the connection between environmentalism and anti-capitalism suggests that people's anxiety about preserving nature is also feeding darker forces of the soul. Environmentalism is fuelling modern scapegoating.

In fact, there's nothing new about this connection. Scapegoating has always been about nature and the weather, and about how both affect, and supposedly are affected by, people. Consider the following episodes, diseases and disasters that were blamed on witches in the Middle Ages:

Fungus invasions, insect invasions, worm invasions, toad invasions, cat invasions, rat invasions, animals shrinking, killer jellyfish, alligators in the Thames, avalanches, contaminated blood, blind salmon, blind rabbits, blizzards, shrinking brains, bluetongue (disease of ruminants), Brewer's Droop, the Plague, forest fires, camel deaths, cannibalism, amorous cats, sleeplessness, cold weather, crop failures, cross-breeding animals, cyclones, sick children, sick dogs, droughts, dust spreading, the earth dying, the light dimming, the earth exploding, starvation, soil quality declining, flesh-eating disease, wilting flowers, thick fog, food poisoning, giant snakes, bald hedgehogs, hurricanes, indigestion, itchier poison ivy, super-intelligent lizards, milk production declining, oak trees dying, increasing piracy, increasing prostitution, rabid bats, torrential rain, sheep changing colour, sheep shrinking, spiders getting bigger.

Crikey, they were paranoid in those days! They were indeed. But I confess I've played a trick on you, dear reader. That list is *not* a list of known charges against witches (although it would probably be a pretty accurate one). It is a list of charges against global warming, according to newspaper headlines recorded by John Brignell at www.numberwatch.co.uk. The list I have cited is only a small fraction of all the accusations assembled on Brignell's website. Some of the distinctly modern charges against global warming include: plane crashes, bird strikes on planes, AIDS, bridges collapsing, terrorism, nuclear war, chocolate shortages, ruined golf tournaments, depression, and the death of the Loch Ness Monster.

The global warming agenda has energised anti-capitalism with the force of a fission reaction. Until recent decades, most post-war anti-capitalists were motivated by a sense of grievance and envy – in other words, by soured relationships with their fellow men. These kinds of negative interpersonal motivations were always a major factor in witch-hunting, but not the only factor, nor indeed the most powerful. Above all, witch-hunting was stimulated, like all forms of scapegoating, by a fear of nature. Faced with nature's destructiveness – whether of people or crops, whether through diseases or fearsome weather – people have always sought culprits. Today, the scary notion that the planet is heating up and causing the environment to become increasingly destructive is awakening humanity's atavistic fear of nature, and our atavistic search for culprits. Capitalists, accordingly, are the obvious scapegoats. With their hubristic attempts to meddle in nature using sorcery-like technology, with their baffling jargon and ritualised meetings, with their status within society as insiders who are also outsiders (they live among us but they trade with *them*), with their networks of contacts throughout society, with their evident strength and influence, and with their supposed disregard for the future of "our children", capitalists make apt 'Enemies of the People'.

Ever since the environmental movement hit upon the idea of catastrophic anthropogenic global warming, the demonisation of capitalism has advanced in waves, triggered by pronouncements from some of the most powerful figures on Earth – including, as usual, the Pope. It's a positive feedback loop. The more we learn to fear nasty capitalists, the more we hunker down and look searchingly towards our leaders, who, in turn, encourage us to fear nasty capitalists. The media, too, is ever willing to disseminate attention-grabbing scare stories, and to piously distribute blame. In 2013, when scientists reported that an asteroid was approaching Earth, CNN's anchor Deb Feyerick asked earnestly: 'is this an effect, perhaps, of global warming?'

The logic of scapegoating explains why environmentalism has slotted itself so effortlessly into the mindset of anti-capitalism, and vice versa. Envy and a fear of nature are natural bedfellows insofar as they both point in the direction of unwarranted blame, and insofar as they both inspire a groupish hostility towards individuals.

At this point, in my mind's ear, I can hear dismayed readers crying, "when it comes to the environment, the majority *is* right; the blaming of capitalism *is* warranted; capitalists *are* destroying the planet; anyone who denies this fact is a 'climate change denier', on a par with a Holocaust denier". I'm not so sure – and neither are trailblazing authors such as Christopher Booker, Matt Ridley and James Delingpole. In fact, I'm increasingly sure that, when it comes to the environment, 'what's good is bad, what's bad is good', to borrow a Bob Dylan lyric (from another context). In my experience, environmentalists display all the same character flaws that are found among anti-capitalists: the hypocrisy, the commitment to backfiring policies, the impulse to control society, the tragic herd mentality, the self-deception, the indifference to reality. Meanwhile, capitalism is more environmentally friendly than people give it credit for.

The first hint that the governance isn't always greener on the other side can be seen in the hypocrisy displayed by environmentalists. Like the rest of us, environmentalists drive cars, shop at the supermarket (where they lie through their teeth about having 'too much choice'), deposit their money in banks, use electricity, consume limited resources, have children, and so on. And, unlike the rest of us, environmentalists organise thousands of conferences requiring millions of taxpayer-funded delegates to fly all over the world and congregate in heated buildings where a discussion ensues about the evils of flying and heating. In short, environmentalists are complicit in almost every sin of which capitalism is the alleged author. Just as Cleanthes invited the self-styled sceptic Philo to leave by the window in Hume's dialogues, I once challenged an ardent environmentalist to move his wife and kids out of his house and into a tent once our conversation was over. He didn't. The relentless complicity of environmentalists in the alleged crimes of capitalism entails that capitalists are not exclusively deserving of the blame of which environmentalists speak; in other words, capitalists are scapegoats.

Moreover, many of the accusations made by environmentalists against their capitalist scapegoats are questionable, to say the least. For a start, those accusations are dubious in point of logic. We are warned by environmentalists about longer winters, shorter winters, glaciers melting, glaciers forming, seas becoming more salty, seas becoming less salty, floods worsening, droughts worsening, people dying, people overpopulating the planet, clouds thinning, clouds thickening, and so on. In 2000, climate scientist David Viner reported gloomily that soon 'children just aren't going to know what snow is'; a decade later, when Britain was blanketed in snow, environmental campaigner George Monbiot had a similar but completely different message: 'that snow outside is what global warming looks like.' The many mutually contradictory doomsday prognostications that issue forth from the environmentalists cannot all be true.

And we know that environmentalists have been wrong in the past. During the inaugural Earth Day event in 1970, ecologist Kenneth Watt predicted that the planet would be 'eleven degrees colder in the year 2000', Senator Gaylord Wilson claimed that by 1995 'between 75 and 85 per cent of all the living species of animals will be extinct', while biologist George Wald warned that 'civilisation will end within 15 to 30 years unless immediate action is taken against problems facing mankind'. That same decade, hundreds of green lobby groups successfully agitated for a ban against the anti-malarial pesticide DDT, a compound that, in her popular book *Silent Spring*, Rachel Carson implied would cause a cancer 'epidemic' in humans. Decades later, most environmental groups have admitted they were wrong about DDT. Though it should have been used more carefully than it was – by spraying it on the inside walls of houses rather than over wide areas where it was dangerous to birds – its worldwide ban caused millions of preventable deaths. As for the predictions of the Agenda 21 quote with which I opened this section, Matt Ridley, in his book *The Rational Optimist*, summarises what actually happened next: 'The following decade saw the sharpest decrease in poverty, hunger, ill health and illiteracy in human history.'

Again and again, the warnings of environmentalists have turned out to be exaggerated or inaccurate. Polar bear numbers are increasing, not decreasing. Acid rain did not kill or even damage forests, as confirmed by a ten-year study in the US. Global vegetation cover is increasing, not decreasing (partly due to the accumulation of CO_2 in the atmosphere). Fracking has been carried out in Britain and the US for decades and has proven safe and effective. Sperm counts aren't declining. Oil spills in the oceans are down. In Europe and the US, the air is getting cleaner, as are the rivers, lakes and seas. Nuclear radioactivity levels have declined since the 1960s, and now account for less than one per cent of natural background radiation. The main driver of the alarming global rate of species extinctions is not modern prosperity but the spread of invasive species. 'Chemicals' haven't shortened our lifespans, quite the opposite. Nuclear disasters have proved less disastrous than feared; the latest estimate is that 4000 people, not the originally predicted 500,000, will die of cancer in the Chernobyl region (and probably no one will die following the reactor leak at Fukushima in Japan, an event that, tellingly, overshadowed the death of 20,000 people in the tsunami that caused the leak). Our growing global population – which, incidentally, is growing at a decreasing rate – has been accompanied by improving health and prosperity among the world's poorest people. We're certainly not running out of space: you could fit the entire world's population into a city the size of the state of Texas. Extreme weather events haven't become more common, and (thanks to the wealth and power afforded to us by capitalism) the global probability of dying in a drought, flood or storm is at its lowest level ever. And sea levels haven't increased 'by twenty feet', as Al Gore predicted in 2006 they would 'in the near future'.

Yes, when it comes to the most doom-laden theory of all – that the planet is heating up due to an accumulation of manmade CO_2 in the atmosphere – we should exercise a degree of cynicism. Meteorologists can't predict the weather a few weeks in advance let alone a few decades, and neither can climate scientists. None of them predicted the global warming 'hiatus' which occurred between 1998 and 2013, when CO_2 levels continued to rise but global temperatures stubbornly plateaued. And none of the climate scientists have so far been correct in their predictions of the so-called 'feedback effects' of global warming. Feedback effects refer to the idea that global warming-induced events (e.g. glaciers melting, changes in cloud cover) will cause global warming to intensify, leading to a runaway process that will send global temperatures soaring, with all the devastation that entails (e.g. sea levels rising twenty feet, millions of 'climate refugees', ecosystems destroyed, widespread famine). So far, it's all quiet on the weather front. Indeed, many sceptics argue that the feedback effects of global warming will be *negative*, meaning that the warming will tend to slow its own rate down.

Of course, I don't claim to be in a position to be able to judge fairly what the weather will or won't do. But I *can* recognise that environmentalists aren't always judging fairly; their shiftiness is made plain in exposés such as Christopher Booker's *The Real Global Warming Disaster* and James Delingpole's *The Little Green Book of Eco-Fascism*. I can recognise, for instance, that the environmentalists' rhetorical fixation on Antarctica is rather fishy; you can say pretty much anything you want about such a vast and remote continent; no one is likely to be able to contradict you. And I can recognise when climate scientists are hiding or downplaying their own inconvenient truths, such as the fact that global sea levels have been rising since the end of the last ice age 12,000 years ago, or the fact that there was a 'Medieval Warm Period' around 1000 AD, when there were no engines polluting the air with CO_2 yet global temperatures were hotter than today – vineyards grew in the north of England – suggesting that man's economic activities are not the only contributor to global warming. (As Delingpole summarises: 'Nothing that the climate has been doing in our lifetime is in any way more dramatic than anything it has been doing in the last 10,000 or so years.') Relatedly, I can recognise that environmental science has paid insufficient attention to one of the most enduring and obvious influences on global temperatures – the sun. Henrik Svensmark, for instance, was marginalised by the climate science establishment for his pioneering work on 'cosmoclimatology'.

Indeed, I can recognise the shallowness of the environmentalists' emphasis on the 'consensus' of climate scientists. For a start, the much-quoted claim that '97 per cent of the world's climate scientists agree that global warming is man-made' is highly questionable. The figure came from an online survey of just 77 people, a survey with a simplistic format that wasn't capable of reflecting the variety of views among climate scientists about the extent and significance of man's influence on the climate. Moreover, even when there is a consensus in science, that doesn't make everybody right; the focus should always be on the data and the facts, not the fashions. After all, if consensus were paramount in science, Einstein would have remained a patent clerk, and we'd all believe in the existence of phlogiston. Similarly, the emphasis placed by environmentalists on 'peer-reviewed' science is misguided. If Einstein's peers, as opposed to a single editor, had had the final say on the four groundbreaking papers he submitted to the *Annalen der Physik* in 1905 (his 'miracle year') then the prevailing (incorrect) theories might have prevailed. That, indeed, is precisely what is happening today on Wikipedia, where legions of environmentalists are engaged in an editing campaign designed to smother outlying views on climate change.

And I can recognise when climate scientists themselves admit that they are not so much interested in the truth as interested in the pursuit of an agenda. In 2009, thousands of emails and computer files were leaked from the University of East Anglia's Climate Research Unit, one of the most influential environmental science establishments in the world. Many of the 'Climategate' emails conveyed a distinct impression that their authors were not being entirely impartial as scientists. Kevin Trenberth was caught announcing, in relation to the recent global warming hiatus: 'The fact is that we can't account for the lack of warming at the moment and it is a travesty that we can't.' Head of the Unit, Phil Jones, admitted to massaging data: 'I've just completed Mike's Nature trick of adding in the real temps to each series for the last 20 years (ie from 1981 onwards) and from 1961 for Keith's to hide the decline.' Jones was also caught threatening to distort the International Panel on Climate Change's report – the most authoritative climate science and policy document in the world – by excluding dissenting voices and, in effect, misrepresenting the scientific literature: 'I can't see either of these papers being in the next IPCC report. Kevin and I will keep them out somehow – even if we have to redefine what the peer review literature is!' Meanwhile, Ben Santer, who was then a researcher at the CRU, fantasised about imposing some even tougher sanctions on a well-known climate sceptic: 'Next time I see Pat Michaels at a scientific meeting, I'll be tempted to beat the crap out of him. Very tempted.'

Other environmental scientists are less covert when it comes to the influence of their political outlook on their work. For instance, geographer Mike Hulme has admitted openly that 'self-evidently dangerous climate change will not emerge from a normal scientific process of truth-seeking'. I invite you to pause to consider how perverse that statement is. Hulme is telling us that science is about making a point. It's the same barmy claim previously made by the mid-twentieth century Soviet scientist Trofim Lysenko, who, together with his followers in Russia and China, argued that the scientific process should be manipulated so that it reaches ideologically correct conclusions.

A common way in which climate scientists try to make their point is through computer modelling. Researchers build a programme that supposedly represents the earth's meteorological system, then feed in various data and see what the model predicts. Most of the doomsday prognostications of environmentalists are based on this methodology. But its flaws are obvious: if you build the model, you can make it say whatever you like. The most flamboyant example of this data gerrymandering can be seen in a misleading graph which became an emblem of the green movement. The 'hockey stick' graph was so called because it shows a historical temperature trajectory that culminates in a blade-shaped uptick around the turn of the nineteenth century. The graph seemed to be compelling evidence of runaway anthropogenic global warming, until sceptics observed that this 'evidence' was based on an algorithm that generated a hockey stick-shaped graph more than 99 per cent of the time, whatever data you fed into it.

Meanwhile, the climate scientists' computer models generally can't be tested anyway – their predictions are mostly about the future, not the present. Delingpole has accused the climate establishment of the 'highly unscientific practice of rejecting empiricism in favour of grand universal doom theories'.

Of course, not all climate scientists who are environmentalists are entirely comfortable about abandoning the 'normal scientific process of truth-seeking'. For some scientists, a commitment to both science and environmentalism amounts to a moral dilemma. The late Stephen Schneider, Professor of Environmental Biology at Stanford University, noted:

> On the one hand as scientists we are ethically bound to the scientific method [...]. On the other hand we need [...] to capture the public's imagination. So we have to offer up scary scenarios, make simplified, dramatic statements, and make little mention of any doubts we might have.

It is hard to see how any campaign could be genuinely helped by simplification, melodrama and uncritical zealousness. But it is easy to see how the green scientists' pantomimic approach has captured the public's imagination, and therefore set the electoral agenda. As the environmental PR firm Futerra Sustainability Communications explains: 'changing behaviour by disseminating information doesn't always work, but emotions and visuals do.' In the end, the climate scientists' dilemma is no dilemma at all. A scientist is *not* bound to the scientific method if he is ultimately bound to peddle untruth by way of 'emotions and visuals'.

Naturally, when science misleads, it leads to campaigns that mislead. In 1986, Patrick Moore, who was one of the founding members of Greenpeace, quit the organisation, claiming that it had 'abandoned scientific objectivity in favour of political agendas'. He was right – as proved by the conduct of his successors. In 2009, when Greenpeace Director Gerd Leipold was questioned on the BBC regarding false claims his colleagues had made about the melting of Arctic ice, Leipold all but conceded that Greenpeace had lied: 'we're not ashamed of emotionalising issues.'

Well, the rest of us should be worried. Lysenkoism led to the starvation of millions of Russians and Chinese, whose governments took seriously his agricultural theories, which included ideological claims such as that weeds could spontaneously transmute into grain crops, and that seeds should be sown in clusters to promote solidarity and cooperation among the plants. Today, similarly, when scientists and campaigners aim to mislead us about environmental issues, we end up with governance that misleads – literally leading us into error. We are led, indeed, to shoot the environmentalists in the foot. The epistemic nonchalance – arrogance, even – of green campaigners prompts the state to intervene in the natural world in ways that are at best ineffectual and at worst positively harmful to the planet and to people (especially the poor). Consider what would happen if you tried to influence a complex process you knew little about – say, managing a farm. Most likely your contribution wouldn't be positive but ineffectual or harmful. In fact, even ineffectual measures are harmful; wantonly wasting time and money is neglectful. Expensively pointless environmental schemes divert money away from more prosaic but effective ways to protect the natural world, such as efforts to conserve species and clean up pollution and rubbish.

Environmentalism past and present is littered with policies that have been less than friendly to the environment. A prime example is wind farming. On the surface, the proliferation of wind farms throughout Britain looks like an enlightened development, even though – most people would agree – wind turbines are ugly and spoil countryside views. But even from a functional point of view, wind power doesn't measure up. Wind farms make scant difference to CO_2 production, and may even increase it, because they require back-up power stations running on 'spinning reserve', that is, ready to take the strain when the wind stops blowing, which is a frequent occurrence. The Telegraph has reported that by 5pm on one Thursday in 2013, a wind farm on Anglesey had registered just 0.001 per cent of its maximum output capacity – enough to make a few cups of tea. At average performance levels, it takes thousands of turbines to supply the same amount of energy as a 1200 MW coal-fired or nuclear power station. Alternatively, when the wind is blowing too hard, turbines can cause the opposite problem – power surges, leading to destabilisation of the grid. Sometimes the government has to pay energy companies to switch turbines *off*.

When that happens, at least it is good news for

flying creatures; more than 25 million bats and birds are fatally thumped out of the sky each year by wind turbines in the US alone. Many other green policies are no less harmful to nature. Biofuel plantations have destroyed the habitats of orangutans and other rainforest creatures. Solar farms, likewise, destroy habitats (and, in some cases, exploit water sources for cooling), while the manufacturing of solar panels generates biohazardous chemicals. The battery cells in electric cars contain large quantities of lithium, which is procured by one of the least eco-friendly forms of mining. And hydropower stations can devastate wildlife; for instance, the oft-proposed £30 billion 'Severn Barrage' scheme in Britain threatens to kill fish and displace birds, and to put an end to one of the county's most amazing natural phenomena, the Severn Bore tidal wave.

Even a strategy as seemingly innocuous as the environmentalists' opposition to 'food miles' can have hidden environmental costs. Locally grown food requires less transportation, but when you factor in the costs of fertilisers and heating, imported food is often more environmentally friendly than food produced at home. There are also environmental costs to 'organic farming', that is, farming which eschews the use of Genetically Modified crops, synthetic fertilisers and pesticides, and various other forms of 'intensification'. Farming intensification leads to higher crop yields, meaning that more food can be grown on less agricultural land, meaning that more land can be left over for wildlife and wilderness.

Perhaps the most harmful of environmental schemes are those that attempt to capture and store CO_2. So-called 'carbon sequestration' is prone to leakages and a build-up of pressure, and has therefore proven expensive and dangerous. A recent report found that the storage of all the CO_2 emissions of an average-sized fossil fuel power station would require an underground reservoir the size of a small US state.

Increasingly, governments are trying to circumvent the costs of carbon sequestration by reducing CO_2 emissions at their source. To this end, the 1992 UN Action Plan ushered in the construction of a 'carbon trading' economic sector, wherein companies trade cash for 'carbon credits', that is, legal permission to produce a specified volume of CO_2. However, the regulation of carbon trading requires massive expenditure on the part of governments, while businesses are likewise diverted away from potentially more productive opportunities. In 2011, the total value of the global carbon trading market reached $176 billion. That's roughly the same as the value of global wheat production. As Delingpole points out, the comparison isn't favourable to environmentalism: 'Wheat provides 20 per cent of the calories consumed by the 7 billion people on the planet. Carbon trading produces nothing of value to anyone.'

Delingpole's heretical statement gets right to the heart of the issue. For most environmentalists, the harms perpetrated against 'the planet' by global warming are so extensive and severe that the curtailment of those harms justifies a large human cost. The problem with this view is that it is too dismissive of the value of human beings, and, as a result, too dismissive of the value of capitalism, thus leading ultimately to an overly pessimistic appraisal of the risks of global warming.

Environmentalists have such a dim view of

mankind, their accusations of wrongdoing often shade into misanthropy. Many times you'll hear green campaigners describe the human race as a 'cancer' or a 'virus' on the earth. When environmentalists display their alleged humanity, less of humanity is supposedly more. Ted Turner has declared that a 'total world population of 250–300 million people, a 95 per cent decline from present levels, would be ideal'. He doesn't say if (or how) he is planning to bring about this drastic decline, but one environmental group thinks it has the answer: the 'Voluntary Extinction Movement'. Founder Les U. Knight has argued that 'Phasing out the human race will solve every problem on Earth, social and environmental'.

There is something strikingly incongruous about an environmental philosophy that construes the human race as a cancer yet doggedly defends the rights of an unborn generation of human beings, and passionately argues for anti-capitalist welfare policies that incentivise wanton reproduction – but I will pass swiftly over these points, as I will pass over the hypocrisy of environmentalists who evidently do not treat themselves or, indeed, their children as a 'cancer'. More important is that environmentalists are often so misanthropic they are blinded to the benefits of capitalism. This is true in the sense that people who are afraid of humanity display a lack of openness when it comes to relating to their fellow men: if you think people are viruses, you're unlikely to seek ways to help and be helped by them, in other words, to trade with them. But there's also a more surprising consequence of the misanthropy of environmentalists. Anti-capitalism blinds people to the ways in which capitalism is beneficial to the environment.

For a start, capitalism promotes some specific mechanisms that reduce the likelihood that people will harm the environment. Private property laws, for instance, motivate landowners to protect the environment; the owners likely don't want to live in an unpleasant place, or see the value of their land reduced Morcovei, in some industries, private ownership can actually lead to increases in some of the natural resources supposedly threatened by capitalism. For instance, commercial silviculture, though much maligned, can lead to an increase in forest cover; the demand for wood means that foresters need wood, so they grow forests. That's why forest cover in Europe and America, and in countries such as India and China (where the resource-hungry middle classes are growing rapidly), is increasing, not decreasing. Furthermore, commercial forest management can also help prevent forest fires. Fishing is another sector where, for similar reasons, private property has beneficial effects on the environment.

Capitalism also protects the environment insofar as a free society – unlike bureaucratic governance – encourages communities to take responsibility for their own affairs. Social capital is good for the environment, because community members typically conclude that they don't want to live in a shared mess, or see the value of their homes decline; local people make an effort to preserve their surroundings. Communities can also exert pressure – through political and consumer channels – on local businesses, leading them to adopt greener practices.

In contrast, the government's efforts to manage the environment are typically conducted by distant, office-bound functionaries who care less about the areas of their jurisdiction than do the locals or individuals who have a more direct stake in those areas. In sneering at people who care about where they live – people who display a so-called 'Not In My Back Yard' attitude – and in quixotically campaigning for the abolition of private property, environmentalists are, in effect, seeking to substitute government indifference for two of the most powerful drivers of environmental protection.

Decision-making by local people as opposed to governments can also lead to a higher level of competence when it comes to protecting the environment. When people are actively engaged in a situation, they are better informed about what they are facing, and when they are better informed they have a better sense of what course of action is worth taking. People who were aware, for instance, of the true costs and benefits of recycling probably wouldn't recycle as much household rubbish as most of us are legally required to today. The process of sorting through the collected rubbish is laborious and expensive, as is – for most recyclables – the process of converting the rubbish back into useful raw materials. Critics have argued that (household waste) recycling, on the whole, actually uses up more resources than it yields. In other words, the critics say, recycling is wasteful; without taxpayer subsidies it would be unaffordable; that is, in effect, taxpayers lose money so as to pay the wages of people who work in the (typically public-private) recycling industry.

Of course, there are some definite environmental benefits to recycling, insofar as we can avoid incinerating rubbish or turning it into landfill. But those benefits are very small. Landfill, for example, is not so bad. It is much cheaper than recycling, and produces methane gas which can piped away for industrial use; and most landfill sites are ultimately turned into parkland. As for the space required for landfill – well, there's plenty of land in the world. Based on the calculations of economist A. Clark Wiseman, John Tierney has reported that there is enough space to store 1000 years' worth of American rubbish on just 0.01 per cent of the nation's available grazing land. Alternatively, incineration is not so bad either. Modern high-temperature 'clean burn' incinerators produce a low level of pollution but enough electricity to power 20,000 homes for a year. So – yes – there is a small environmental cost associated with both landfill and incineration, but this cost has to be set against the high cost of recycling; the money and resources spent on recycling could be spent on environmental work that is much more impactful. This is true even if the critics are wrong, that is, even if recycling sometimes generates more resources than it uses, and thus reduces global resource usage to the extent of the net return. By choosing cheaper waste disposal alternatives, and by investing our money in projects with higher economic returns than recycling, we could use all the extra money to carry out projects with a higher environmental impact than recycling.

Governments have a habit of using taxpayers' money to subsidise expensive green schemes that generate minimal or negative returns and have a minimal or negative impact on the environment. Frightened by the prospect of droughts caused by catastrophic global warming, the Australian government pushed up water bills by spending billions of pounds between 2006 and 2012 on a handful of desalination plants; the Sydney and Victorian plants since their construction have spent much of their time in a mothballed state, imposing continued expenses on the taxpayer.

A similar level of wastefulness can be seen throughout the government-subsidised green energy sector. By forcing us to pay higher taxes or higher energy bills, by forcing us to derive a lower return from our money than we would have accrued from investing it in conventional energy, and by achieving at best a low environmental impact, 'green' energy policies are often wasteful. And, of course, the wastefulness of green energy hurts the poor above all; fuel poverty kills an estimated 7800 people a year in Britain, mostly among the elderly population, while, in general, the squandering of public money hurts those taxpayers most who can least afford to pay.

Government-subsidised 'biofuels', in particular, have been a disaster. Land allocated to biofuels could have been used for food production. By pushing up the price of food, biofuels lead to starvation – especially in Africa. Delingpole has even suggested that biofuels may have caused the civil wars in Libya and Syria, by causing the food price inflation that provoked the food riots that triggered the Arab Spring that started the conflicts.

In contrast to the wastefulness of green governance, the greenest thing about capitalism is its efficiency. Markets usually perform tasks more efficiently than governments, because businesses that don't operate efficiently soon stop existing, whereas governments operate under no such pressure. Efficiency is environmentally friendly because it achieves results through lower resource usage. In other words: capitalism gives you more bang for your buck. Economists often talk about the 'opportunity cost' borne by taxpayers when governments spend money; the 'cost' refers to the things that we *didn't* get to spend our money on. Private spending has an opportunity cost too, of course, but when it comes to green governance – as for most forms of governance – the opportunity cost is often much higher than the returns we receive from the government. For instance, Verso Economics found that for every green job created by government investment in Britain, 3.7 jobs were killed in the real economy.

"But" – the environmentalists will object – "we can't just do nothing, leaving capitalism to run amok! The problems of global warming, global resource shortages, and an exploding global population are too serious to ignore. And these problems are too big for local communities. Only coordinated national and international action will suffice." In the face of these global problems, so it goes, it is apparently perfectly reasonable to forcibly divert taxpayers' money away from conventional forms of economic activity. Presumably that's why Britain's Climate Change Act of 2008, which was drafted by Baroness Worthington, a former employee of Friends of the Earth, legally committed the government to implementing cuts in CO_2 so drastic that they cannot possibly be achieved by the planned date of 2050 without shutting down most of the economy.

A cynic, of course, would point out how convenient, not *in*convenient, global problems are to the agenda of anti-capitalists. Global problems are so huge they require bureaucracies at the national or international level, and being so huge the problems can never be grasped with complete accuracy; this might inspire humility in some people, but, for anti-capitalists, unquantifiable problems are an opportunity for unaccountable spin and duplicity. Global problems are also an opportunity to subdue the average man of average intelligence, who realises he can't possibly cope with such matters; he defers, naturally, to the benevolent leaders who claim to know best. Moreover, because such huge problems can never truly be beaten – there is no 'normal' global temperature, no possibility of entirely eliminating waste, no possibility of discovering energy without costs or limits – environmentalism provides anti-capitalists with a never-ending excuse for exercising ever-increasing control. Perhaps above all, global problems furnish anti-capitalists with a mission that befits their self-image, that is, as saviours of the planet and the human race.

Well, capitalism is also pretty good at saving the planet and the human race – better than anti-capitalism, in fact. For one thing, CO_2 is not *all* bad; it's good for coral and plankton, not to mention plants and trees. And CO_2-induced global warming will likewise have plenty of beneficial effects, summarised by Matt Ridley as follows: 'fewer winter deaths; lower energy costs; better agricultural yields; probably fewer droughts; maybe richer biodiversity.' Professor Richard Tol of Sussex University has argued that the various beneficial effects of global warming will outweigh the negative effects, at least for quite a while. His calculations are based on a global temperature increase of up to 2.2°C, a threshold the International Panel on Climate Change believes won't be reached until around 2080.

And the good news won't end there. If, in the

aggregate, the impacts of global warming become negative around the turn of the next century, then the continuation of capitalism in the meantime will have equipped our descendants to deal with the situation. After all, the whole basis of climate alarmism is that *anthropogenic global warming will be a concomitant of continued economic growth*. In the most likely scenario (based on Matt Ridley's summary of various expert estimates), by 2100 global warming will have caused a 1.3 per cent reduction in the incomes of our grandchildren, but prior to that reduction their incomes will be at least three times that of ours. In other words, global warming will make our grandchildren 195 per cent richer than us as opposed to 200 per cent richer than us. Ridley's conclusion is scathing:

> And yet world leaders are prepared to adopt and defend policies that hurt poor people today in order to try to avert this very slight pay cut for the very wealthy of tomorrow. In what universe does this entitle them to occupy the moral high ground?

As for our grandchildren, what will they make of all this? Richard Lindzen of MIT has speculated:

> Future generations will wonder in bemused amazement that the early twenty-first century's developed world went into hysterical panic over a globally averaged temperature increase of a few tenths of a degree, and, on the basis of gross exaggerations of highly uncertain computer projections combined into implausible chains of inference, proceeded to contemplate a roll-back of the industrial age.

Future generations will be bemused precisely because of how much they stand to lose not from global warming but from the anti-capitalist panic over global warming. Especially for the world's poorest people, capitalism has plenty more good news in store. Continuing the trajectory of the last century, trade and economic growth will lift more and more developing countries out of poverty. In Africa, South America and the Asian subcontinent, billions of people will soon enjoy the lifestyle to which we in the West have become accustomed. This thought terrifies environmentalists. But the rest of us needn't worry. The industrialisation and ensuing enrichment of the developing world will lead to what epidemiologists call a 'demographic transition', that is, the crossing of a threshold at which poor people become so rich that they stop having so many children. People stop reproductively overcompensating when their children are unlikely to die young, and the population soon stabilises (or declines slightly), just as Western populations did over the last century. Global capitalism will bring about a global demographic transition – in other words, a world population that is wealthier and more static.

As for concerns about global resource shortages – including shortages of land – capitalism cannot make the finite infinite, but, by making our technologies more efficient, capitalism can make the finite go increasingly far, such as in the example of farming intensification. As Ridley argues, there is every reason to expect tomorrow's global population to be richer, healthier and happier than today's. Moreover, by promoting innovation, capitalism can help the human race discover and utilise new resources; as the saying goes, 'the stone age didn't end for lack of stone'. We, like our ancestors, simply cannot imagine what resources and technologies lie in store for us, but we can rely on entrepreneurs and markets to make any new opportunities increasingly available and useful to us. Even in the doomsday scenario – in which there are simply no better resources available to us in the future than those we already know about today – capitalism will still be preferable to anti-capitalism. Amid scarcity, it is *more* vital, not less, for human beings to trade, to innovate, to become more efficient. That's why environmentalists are so misguided when they argue that "a finite planet can't sustain infinite growth". Growth is *not* a measure of how much stuff is taken from the planet. Growth is a measure of productivity, and productivity is almost entirely a measure of the extent to which people are benefitting from trade (without trade, each of us would be restricted to Robinson Crusoe-levels of productivity). Trade can – and should be allowed to – benefit us indefinitely, whatever resources we possess.

Above all, capitalism nurtures the environment by giving us the wherewithal to engage in and support green initiatives. When your kids are slowly being killed by parasitic worms, and your house is being eaten by termites, the plight of 'the planet' doesn't seem quite so urgent. In contrast, capitalism has furnished us with lives of luxury and ease, with time and resources to spend on caring about other species and the natural world. Capitalism also affords us the luxury of green governance (whether genuine or otherwise); we willingly elect politicians who promise to deploy our surpluses in the task of protecting nature. A combination of wealth and enlightened governance has, for instance, enabled us in Britain to allocate around 12 per cent of our land to legally protected National Parks.

Businesses likewise can afford to respect the environment the more their costs are minimised and their profits maximised by the increased efficiency wrought by capitalism. Sometimes, indeed, businesses are in the vanguard of environmental protection. This was nicely demonstrated by sceptic Julian Simon during a public debate with environmentalist Hazel Henderson in 1996. Henderson produced a graph showing that in London there had been a decline in pollution levels since the late 1950s. She attributed this decline to London's Clean Air Act of 1956. But Simon had a graph of his own up his sleeve, revealing that the same decline in pollution continued back as far as 1920. 'If you look at *all* the data', he insisted, 'you can't tell that there was a Clean Air Act at any point'. When you think about it, trends such as the one observed by Simon are not so surprising. It's not as though without environmental regulations there are no other laws or disincentives discouraging people from harming each other. The cheaper it is for a business to desist from generating pollution, the more foolhardy it is for that business to run the risk of going ahead and being sued by a neighbouring landowner or local community, or – worse – shunned by customers.

Of course, it's not all rosy in the garden of capitalism. If capitalism comprises an upwardly green trajectory overall, then that doesn't mean there are no dips along the way. In particular, environmentalists are correct in pointing out that capitalism itself is more than capable of generating tragedies of the commons. Businesses are forever seeking a competitive edge;

hence, inevitably some will pursue individual gains at the expense of collective harms. One such form of collective harm is environmental damage, for instance in the form of pollution, overfishing, overfarming, habitat destruction (leading to extinction), or simply aesthetic damage to the natural world. (I am reluctant to include the 'exploitation' of resources on this list: as a general rule, it is hardly in everyone's interests to leave valuable resources where they are.)

Environmentalists are also correct in pointing out that capitalism has a self-destructive streak manifested in a series of tragedies of the commons that occur within our economic and social interactions. Consider the modern scourge of manipulative marketing. There's nothing wrong with marketing per se (quite the contrary; people would be more tempted by rapaciousness if they weren't able to get ahead by marketing their goods). But manipulative marketing *is* collectively harmful. When businesses try to gain an advantage over one another by spending money on advertising campaigns that use emotional cajoling to persuade people to spend more money than is good for them on products or services that are likewise not good for them, the whole of society is harmed – by the effects of the adverts, and by the resources wasted, whether on creating the adverts or fulfilling the manipulated consumer demand.

Many other aspects of modern life can, similarly, be construed as tragedies of the commons. For instance: the domination of our lives by glowing screens, i.e. TVs, computers and smartphones; our culture of cynical litigiousness; the saturation of our diets by obesity-causing sugar that has been sneakily implanted into seemingly innocuous food products; the proliferation of guns in the US; the relentless promotion (especially by sports broadcasters) of gambling; our culture of binge drinking; the fashion industry's infantilising influence on the aspirations of billions of people; the problem of traffic congestion (caused by private cars) in cities; the tendency of bankers to enrich themselves inordinately by overexploiting financial reserves; the empty and dangerous populism of politicians; and the preponderance of sensationalism, titillation and scaremongering in the media. (For the details of each tragedy, I direct the reader to my essay 'The Common Bad', which is freely available from www.benirvine.co.uk.)

Together, these economic and social tragedies could be described as 'tragedies of coarseness', that is, tragedies in which people achieve social or economic advantages within the law but at the (collective) expense of sacrificing gentler, healthier, more convivial ways of living. In turn, coarse people treat the natural world coarsely – hence, environmental damage can be counted as another tragedy of coarseness. Environmentalists are right in pointing all this out. But they are wrong in their proposed remedy. Anti-capitalist policies only serve to exacerbate tragedies of coarseness. When businesses and citizens are financially squeezed by scapegoating, when people are carelessly incentivised by welfarism, and when businesses compete wastefully with each other to acquire state funding, they succumb more readily to the gains of coarseness. We've already encountered this phenomenon in chapter 11, when we saw how a scapegoated business is less likely to pay its taxes, treat and pay its staff well, train an apprentice, employ someone out of decency or loyalty, strive for quality not superficial appeal, charge an honest price, provide a friendly 'human' service to customers, or patronise local arts. These are all tragedies of coarseness, and all are exacerbated by anti-capitalism. Similarly, the tendency of individuals to hoard money and evade or avoid taxes is a tragedy of coarseness made worse when capitalism is scapegoated.

Anti-capitalism exacerbates tragedies of coarseness by undermining the mechanisms by which capitalism itself limits those tragedies. In the case of the environment, we have seen how anti-capitalism undermines private property, thus reducing the influence of people who protect or cultivate that part of the environment which they own. We've also seen how anti-capitalism undermines wealth, thus reducing capitalism's scope for resourcefully combating, via governance or other means, its own environmental harms. And we've seen how anti-capitalism undermines communities, thus undermining people's desire to protect their local environment.

This latter example is vividly demonstrated in the work of the late economist Elinor Ostrom, who showed that people are adept at solving environmental tragedies when the scope of those tragedies is local. Problems such as localized overfishing, habitat destruction and overfarming are frequently solved by spontaneous arrangements made by local people. Indeed, Ostrom noted, these arrangements are often undermined when the state wades in with legislation. Moreover, by undermining communities' efforts to solve tragedies at the local level, the government usually simultaneously undermines its own efforts to solve similar tragedies on a larger, societal scale. In other words: an aggregation of communally solved local tragedies is usually more effective in solving tragedies at the societal level than the government's attempts to solve tragedies at that level by wading in heavy-handedly at the local level. There is an interesting parallel here with Friendly Societies, in that these communities spontaneously solved the local 'tragedy' of bogus welfare claims, before being undermined by a state welfare system within which fraud became entrenched. The moral is: when anti-capitalist governance undermines social capital, the result is a tragedy that operates both locally and societally.

Communities can mitigate the tragedy of the environment not just through solving specific local tragedies but by encouraging people to find meaning in their lives in ways that don't exert a heavy toll on the environment. In communities, we sing songs around the proverbial campfire, we perform plays, we recite poetry, we paint and enjoy pictures, we play sports and games, we eat together, we dance together, we attend meetings, we care for each other – none of which makes a large contribution to local or societal-level environmental tragedies.

Similarly, communities are also crucibles for mitigating the other tragedies of coarseness, and this either directly or – by making us less coarse – indirectly benefits the environment. The more social capital we enjoy, the less time we spend staring at glowing screens; the less we drive our cars (and the more we ride our bikes); the more we are motivated by conviviality rather than the siren song of manipulative marketers; the less litigiously we solve our disputes; the more we prepare healthy meals for each other; the less we feel the need to be armed; the less we feel the need to gamble, get drunk, or show off fashionable clothes and possessions; the less of our money we make available to bankers; the less we pay attention to all the doom and gloom and banality in the media; the more we decentralise politics, thereby debunking the demagogic claims of politicians; and the less we partake, whether via our businesses or as individuals, in the tragedies of coarseness mentioned in chapter 11.

In all of this, communities can also help foster a form of openness that dissuades people from contributing to societal-level tragedies. One such tragedy, of course, is inter-communal violence, the prevalence of which was much higher prior to the advent of capitalism. Over the course of millennia, the tendency of communities to engage in mutual raiding – to seek one-sided gains through violence while losing out overall through mutual destruction – has gradually been displaced by the tendency of communities to reap the mutual gains of trade. This process of pacification has been driven partly through governments imposing law and order on their subjects, and partly through the cultivation within communities of a spirit of openness – openness to trading with strangers rather than killing them.

But there is also an enhanced form of openness that can be cultivated by communities. As well as choosing social capital over coarseness, in communities we may also resolve to act in such a way as to minimise the incidence of coarseness within wider society. With our reputations to protect – reputations for community-spiritedness, for eschewing coarseness locally – and with our own internalised communal values, we're less likely to be coarse towards strangers or to encourage them to behave coarsely. We become open to strangers in such a way that we help to minimise tragedies at the societal level. This attitude is particularly significant in our working lives, when we can refuse to profit from coarseness.

Openness to minimising societal-level tragedies of coarseness is not a common attitude today – not as common, perhaps, as it once was. This attitude could be called wide openness (to differentiate it from the more basic form of openness that leads people to trade with each other). Imagine the thought process of a man who decides to trade with a stranger. The man might think: *I'm open to the mutual gains we can enjoy through exchange rather than killing each other*. Now imagine the thought process of a community-spirited man who decides to minimise societal-level tragedies of coarseness. This man might think: *I'm open to the gains of trade, and, moreover, I'm wide open to the mutual gains of reducing coarseness in wider society; for example, I don't want the person I trade with to suffer from pollution or to gamble irresponsibly any more than I want to people in my own community to do so*. Today, this attitude of wide openness is found mainly within 'social enterprises'; these are businesses that heroically aim to make money while declining to inflict tragic harms on society, and while actively pursuing environmental or charitable goals. More businesses would be social enterprises if capitalism were scapegoated less.

Environmentalists are correct in construing environmental abuse – and other forms of coarseness – as tragedies of the commons. But between wide openness and environmentalism there is a gulf, a vast canyon of ideology. Wide openness, after all, is a form of capitalism. It could be called social capitalism. A socially

capitalist economy is replete with nurturing communities, communities that foster not only the openness
that capitalism is built on, but the wide openness that
steers capitalism away from environmental depredation and other forms of coarseness. Environmentalists, in contrast, claim to value wide openness but
they are not even open enough to trade with strangers,
let alone to care about societal-level tragedies. The
green rhetoric of 'act locally, think globally' is deeply
bogus. It says less about communities caring for the
planet and humanity, and more about a fear of
strangers and a fear of nature, about communities
hunkering down, looking searchingly towards state
authority, wishing – impossibly – that the government
would impose social and environmental harmony, and
wealth, upon us.

Of course, wide openness has limits too. As
communism has demonstrated, you cannot attempt to
solve the problems of all human beings all at once
without becoming grotesquely inhuman and inhumane.
But in aiming to minimise societal-level tragedies
whilst not resorting to dangerous fantasies of utopian
anti-capitalist governance, the attitude of wide
openness points distantly towards an intriguing new
possibility for combating those tragedies. It is a
possibility that environmentalists, because they fail to
recognise the benefits of capitalism, are simply blind
to. The possibility is best expressed by way of a
question that nobody yet knows how to begin to
answer, myself included: *through non-governmental
means, how can we can we retain the benefits of
widespread monetary exchange, whilst also factoring
into the prices of our goods and services the extent to
which those goods and services cause or diminish*

tragedies of the commons?

Until such time as an answer to that question is found and put into effect – until, perhaps, technologists develop a clever new currency that is sensitive to tragedies of the commons – capitalism will remain prone to tragedies of coarseness. But capitalism also promotes responsibility, including the responsibility that individuals feel towards their jobs, their finances, their property, their communities, their local area, and even their society. And responsibility, in one guise or another, keeps tragedies of coarseness in check, as does the wealth that capitalism generates, which dampens the temptations of coarseness and enables us to invest in preventing or redressing environmental harms. Because environmentalists don't trust such imperfect solutions, they give up. They acquiesce in anti-capitalism, a trajectory of guaranteed failure. They drag society back in the direction of mutual universal murder. In this way, they choose to contribute to the severest tragedy of all, rather than making an effort to mitigate the – more manageable – tragedies of coarseness. Indeed, in choosing the severest tragedy, environmentalists worsen the tragedies of coarseness. The more a society is shorn of wealth, property and wide-open communities the more coarsely it behaves, and the more coarsely it treats the natural world. And the more a society wastes its wealth on unscientific green governance, which often backfires, the more the natural world bears the brunt once again. Scapegoated capitalism, in its coarseness, provokes environmentalists into blaming capitalism for environmental problems that are either exacerbated or caused by environmentalism.

In all of this, environmentalists are fortified by self-deception. They know subconsciously of the superiority of capitalism to anti-capitalism – their hypocritical behaviour demonstrates this. They know that their favoured policies and civic failings exacerbate capitalism's tragedies of coarseness – the sabotaging of capitalism's moral ascendency is precisely what environmentalists intend to achieve. So – to avoid the shame of what they know – environmentalists lie to themselves; they tell themselves consciously that it is they, not capitalists, who are fostering social and environmental harmony. And environmentalists protest too much, as demonstrated by their unstinting beatification of the natural world, a world that – as we all know only too well – can be cruel as well as wonderful.

Self-deception explains why you can't have a reasonable discussion with an environmentalist. In my experience, it is simply impossible to get an environmentalist to admit to any of the benefits of capitalism, or to recognise that the wealth generated by capitalism can help us to minimise environmental harms. The more rationally you defend capitalism, the more irrationally environmentalists resist the truth, precisely because they know they're wrong. They use all the obfuscatory methods characteristic of anti-capitalists and other self-deceivers – changing the subject, committing logical fallacies, misrepresenting what is being claimed, blustering with outrage, and playing the man not the ball. James Delingpole has noted the latter tendency among environmentalists, having, he says, been subjected to attacks on:

> my physical appearance, my educational back-
> ground, my history of depressive illness, my

performances on TV or radio, my style, my sense of humour [...]. Here's the weird thing though. What these people almost never do is actually engage with the facts and logic of the argument I've presented [...]. When you're taking the flak it means you're over the target.

Perhaps Delingpole should consider himself fortunate. When self-styled 'sceptical environmentalist' Bjørn Lomborg broke ranks with his colleagues, not-so-sceptical environmentalist Mark Lynas threw a cream pie at him, at a book reading event in London. How wasteful – but it was all for a good cause!

Environmentalists are also fortified by the benefits of scapegoating, self-deception being an accessory for the procurement of those benefits. People who scape-goat capitalism for its alleged environmental harms are privy to all the same psychological benefits as any other anti-capitalist, or indeed any other scapegoater, i.e. the pleasures of sadism, guiltlessness, solidarity, cleanliness (green energy is 'clean' not 'dirty'), irresp-onsibility, rationalising suffering, enjoying a release from rumination, and avoiding being scapegoated.

Then there are the economic rewards available to environmentalists, rewards that are considerable, to say the least. Environmentalists insist that we should be afraid of climate sceptics who are supposedly in the pay of "Big Oil", but you seldom hear about Big Green and its very real dangers. Annual US federal and state environmental spending amounts to $44.5 billion, while the EU spent $100 billion on climate change research between 1989 and 2010, and, by 2004, the UN had funded at least 60,000 environ-mental projects.

Meanwhile, in Britain the Climate Change Act is costing an estimated £18.3 billion a year. Taxpayers are, in effect, sponsoring the environmental activists who have infiltrated central and local government (I don't remember voting for these people), where they enjoy salaried positions with job titles such as 'Climate Change Officer', 'Sustainability Policy Advisor' and 'Weevil Excommunication Manager' (OK, I made the last one up, but you get the point).

Government money also finds its way to academics and other intellectuals, among whom, of course, are the many scientist-activists who are engaged in the frenzied planet-saving research otherwise known as consensus building. Venerable scientific organisations have jumped aboard the climate change bandwagon, including the National Academy of Sciences, the Institute of Physics and the Royal Society, the latter having done so with such enthusiasm that dismayed Society member Professor Michael Kelly has accused the organisation of 'not giving advice, but lobbying'. In the US, NASA has also jumped aboard. Between 2006 and 2011, James Hansen, NASA's resident global warming scientist, received cash payments of $1.6 million in relation to his role, plus a salary. Despite this, and despite giving 1400 on-the-job interviews, Hansen had the audacity to allege that he was 'muzzled' by the Bush administration.

Additionally, there are legions of humanities scholars who are paid to offer sanctimonious green musings. Much of what passes as funding for environmental research really pays for what Delingpole describes as:

faux-academic conferences in which climate

scientists, environmentalists and green activists all agree that the global eco crisis is worsening by the day and that the only solution is for more government money to be spent on research and further conferences in which climate scientists, environmentalists and green activists can meet to review how grave the crisis is and how much more government money needs to be spent on it.

Meanwhile, politicians benefit from holding financial interests in green companies; perhaps that's part of the reason why, out of 650 British MPs, only *five* voted against the Climate Change Act. Green energy exemplifies public-private toxicity at its worst. Fat cat energy company bosses profit handsomely from their political alliances, while, in the countryside, wealthy landowners receive huge subsidies for erecting wind farms, much to the chagrin of local communities. Generally speaking, it is easy to see how government-sponsored businesses may become less green, not more. They may become tools for implementing backfiring governmental green policies. Or, government-funded businesses may grow so powerful they become aloof from community life, and therefore obscure, and therefore unaccountable, including in their conduct towards the environment.

The taxpayer-funded BBC has also fallen hook line and sinker for the climate change agenda. So far, our national broadcaster has given not a single iota of airtime to climate sceptics, among whose ranks are the much-loved science presenters David Bellamy and Johnny Ball, who have been summarily removed from the schedules. Countless other media outlets, although not directly funded by the government, continue to toe the climate change line, mostly because most of their audience works for the public sector and generally supports anything that is paid for by taxes and sounds vaguely socialist. The Guardian newspaper, for instance, has thrived by peddling a relentlessly warmist agenda; George Monbiot is paid £67,000 per year for his column, in which he rails against capitalism's environmental destructiveness and 'greed'.

Many charities have likewise pandered to the spirit of the times, and profited handsomely from doing so. The WWF – which these days aspires to 'reduce carbon emissions', 'support sustainable development by integrating the value of environmental resources and biodiversity into national policies', and '[find] ways to share the Earth's resources fairly' – is one of the richest charities in the world, its Chief Executive earning over $450,000 a year. Even London Zoo recently got in on the act, having created a sanctimonious exhibit that reveals 'the most destructive animal in the world'. The exhibit consists in a sign above a wire mesh, the mesh framing passersby as they walk along, making them look like exhibits in a cage. Ah, look, it's human beings! Human beings, with their greed and callousness, are the most destructive animals in the world!

We are certainly witnessing a frenzy of destruction, but perhaps not the one you think. As Delingpole observes: 'Over the last decade or so the institutions have fallen like nine-pins [...] to the point where it's hard now to think of a single august body which hasn't sold its soul, its authority and its intellectual independence to the environmental lobby.' We are witnessing, in other words, a tragedy of the commons, in which increasing numbers of people and organisations are freeloading on the wealth of capitalism while using that wealth to make a negligible or even harmful contribution to humanity and the environment, all in the self-deceptive name of protecting people and the planet. Moreover – to add insult to injury – while environmentalists feed on the wealth of society, particularly the wealth of the poor, they have the audacity to blame the generator of that wealth – capitalism – for their own failings, whether in policy or personal conduct. Such is the benighted nature of modern scapegoating. And – worse – as scapegoated capitalism descends into social and environmental coarseness, the scapegoaters attack it further, and promise to make things better, drawing away ever-more resources in an ever-increasing spiral of destructiveness and degeneration. Environmentalism is a racket.

I hope it is obvious that I am not suggesting that businesses and governments shouldn't bother being green. My whole point is that environmentalism, with its tragic spirit of anti-capitalism, leads to governance that isn't green and therefore to economic activity that isn't green. A coarse society, one that treats the environment coarsely, begins with coarse people taking over the government, setting in train a spiral of mutual coarsening between the government and the public. Tragic governance leads to a tragic society, which leads to tragic governance, and so on.

So what does green governance look like when it isn't coarse, when it isn't anti-capitalistic? In most areas I'm not an expert. But I do know something about government policy relating to cycling, having founded a free magazine that, for five years, promoted the health and environmental benefits of cycling in

London.

As part of this project, I put together a campaign to create a London Underground-style map and network of cycle routes in the capital. There are already thousands of kilometres of cycle routes in London, but they're not mapped or signed properly. The campaign, which is ongoing, is calling for a single 'London Cycle Map' of those routes, accompanied by signs on the streets. I 'discovered' a clever guy called Simon Parker who had created a map design that colour-coded all the cycle routes in London; if the government were to install coloured signs and road markings on the streets corresponding to Parker's design, then cyclists would be able get from more or less anywhere to anywhere in the capital by simply following (in most cases) a maximum of three coloured routes, just as people do when using the London Underground.

I thought Parker's system was ingenious, and potentially life-changing for the millions of Londoners who are not only scared of cycling on the city's traffic-congested main roads but also scared of getting lost in a labyrinth of poorly signed backstreet cycle routes – and, indeed, ending up straying back onto the scary main roads. Over the previous thirty years, the authorities had sensibly chosen (on the whole) to use London's backstreets as cycle routes, where there would be less disruption to other road users, and where most people prefer to cycle anyway (for instance, in Cambridge, where I now live, there are proportionally more cycle journeys undertaken than anywhere else in Britain, and all the roads here are small or medium-sized). If only the authorities in London had finished the job, by mapping and signing the capital's backstreet cycle routes properly! That's what Simon Parker's London Cycle Map promised to do.

There was just one problem: anti-capitalism. Cycle campaigning in London is dominated by environmentalists who argue that London's main roads need better cycling facilities, to help cyclists "reclaim" those roads from cars, taxis, buses and lorries. This campaign strategy is perverse, given that the previous thirty years of traffic engineering measures in London have been designed to stop motor vehicles from rat-running through the backstreets, in other words, to force motor vehicles *onto* the main roads. And the strategy is utterly unrealistic. In a city of ten million people, there will always be a need for major transport arteries, to convey goods and people. Crowbarring cycling facilities onto main roads is a stupid, confrontational idea, one which only anti-capitalists could come up with.

Alas, these days, stupid ideas win the day. Influenced by the (state-subsidised) charity the London Cycling Campaign, the government has created a handful of 'Cycle Superhighways' on some of London's biggest roads, including dual carriageways and flyovers. In their early days, the Cycle Superhighways consisted almost entirely of trails of blue paint daubed along the left-hand edge of some of the most traffic-intense carriageways in the country. In many places, these trails cut directly across slip roads that led off the main carriageway, meaning that cyclists were encouraged to ride straight across the path of vehicles turning left – a manoeuvre which is about as dangerous as it gets on a bike. After the first few routes were completed, the London Cycling Campaign promptly declared (rightly) that they were dangerous, whereupon more money was spent on 'segregating' some sections of the Cycle Superhighways from motor traffic. To date, the Superhighways policy has cost over £50 million, money which has been spent on consultancy fees, legal fees, bureaucracy, strategy reports, marketing, engineering, and more.

All in all, the failings of the Cycle Superhighways have been plain to see: the expense; the disruption to traffic (during and after the building process); the erstwhile danger of the routes (as well as the recklessness of the campaigners' rhetoric of "reclaiming" main roads, a message that goads cyclists onto main roads in general, and into harm's way); and the minimal returns on such a wastefully confrontational project. The campaigners and the government are fond of trumpeting weaselly statistics, e.g. that there has been a 73 per cent rise in cyclists using one route or another. But that pathetic sort of return – 73 per cent of a tiny number added to a tiny number is still a tiny number – must be considered in relation to the opportunity cost of the Cycle Superhighways. Imagine if the campaigners and bureaucrats hadn't picked a fight with capitalism. Imagine if they had concluded that main roads, like airport runways and railway lines, generally aren't sensible places to put cycling infrastructure. Imagine if the government had not had to engage in laborious consultations – and a few legal battles – with businesses affected by the Cycle Superhighways.

Imagine if, instead, the government had created a London Underground-style London Cycle Map corresponding to a network of signed, colour-coded cycle routes on the capital's quieter streets. At an estimated minimum cost of £1.6 million in total, the London Cycle Map and network would have yielded much, much more bang for the taxpayer's buck. People who are currently too scared to cycle in London – people who, when using a Cycle Superhighway, are not reassured by a thin kerb separating them from a 50-tonne truck – could have been reassured by the prospect of following a few quiet, well-signed, well-lit, colour-coded cycle routes. Children, older people, women – all those people who, statistically, are the most reluctant to cycle, especially in London – could have been inspired by the knowledge that they could navigate throughout the whole of the capital by bicycle, safely and simply. That's not just an opportunity cost; it's an opportunity lost.

Who knows what other opportunities for sensible environmental stewardship have been shunned by anti-capitalists in other areas of governance? None the wiser, all that remains for the rest of us is to try to navigate the slew of ideological legislation as best as we can. But anti-capitalism has a nasty habit of making crooks of the sane. A few years ago, the Australian government banned farmers from clearing vegetation from around their homes in the 'bush', an area which is notorious for its raging forest fires. One farmer defied the ban, chopping down a few hundred trees that were growing on his property, and was promptly fined by the government. After the next bush fire, which inevitably came, his was the only house left standing in a two-kilometre area.

As demonstrated by the film *No Pressure*, and indeed by Osama bin Laden's environmentalist rantings, at the heart of environmentalism is a form of bullying that ought to have been left behind in the

Middle Ages. Like medieval scapegoaters, environmentalists convert their fear of nature and their distrust of strangers into an urge to blame and belittle, an urge fuelled by a tragedy of the commons and policed by the dastardliness of self-deception. In environmentalism, the chosen culprits are capitalistic individuals, who are strong enough to bear the burden but weak enough to be subdued. As Delingpole recognises:

> Environmentalism has almost nothing to do with the environment and almost everything to do with control, power, vested interests, religion-grade ideology, money and, ultimately, the totalitarian urge which has possessed half the human species since time immemorial and which continues to make life so much harder than it needs to be for the rest of us.

History suggests we should be especially wary of green-tinged totalitarianism. In the twentieth century, Nazis and communists (in all incarnations of communism) were alike in hankering after a bygone age of agrarian bliss, an age when people were supposedly closer to the land, when the apparatus of modernity had not yet enslaved the nation. Under Nazism and communism, society was dominated by vast government bureaucracies, run by an intelligentsia dedicated to seizing control of the means of production. Under state control, technology would be employed not in oppressing peasants, or scattering them from place to place, but in rooting people back into the soil. And all this would be achieved collectively, through the dedication of forced workers, through the commitment of the nation's scientists to a supposedly noble cause, and through the annihilation of the evil capitalists – the Jews or the Bourgeoisie – who prioritised profits over people.

Yes, believe it or not, Hitler was a vegetarian who favoured alternative medicine. And the Nazis passed legislation for the protection of forests and the banning of experimentation on animals, and were pioneers of organic agriculture. And, yes, Marx envisioned that, following a communist revolution, the people would 'hunt in the morning, fish in the afternoon, rear cattle in the evening, criticise after dinner'. Well, there is plenty to criticise in communism and Nazism, not just in human terms – hundreds of millions dead, murdered by the state or killed in warfare – but in environmental terms too.

The Nazis left behind a continent ravaged by the Scorched Earth policy of the German military. As well as destroying roads and buildings, the retreating Nazi forces spoiled countless sources of food and water. Just as self-deception leads invincibly to a denial of the truth, the totalitarian urge leads inevitably to the tolerance of any cost, whether that cost is borne by people or the planet.

As for communism, the extent of its environmental destructiveness became apparent only when the Iron Curtain began to disintegrate in the late twentieth century. According to statistics cited by Colin Grabow, at the time of its reunification with West Germany, East Germany was ecologically dying, with pollution rife in its lakes, rivers and air, while similar devastation was found throughout the Soviet Bloc, in Poland, Romania, Ukraine, and so on. And, of course, it was in Ukraine that the Chernobyl nuclear accident took place in 1986, when an explosion released about 86 million curies of radioactivity. The Soviets were distinctly casual about harming the environment, their military dumping at least 17 nuclear reactors in the sea, to which the nuclear power industry added an estimated 11,000–17,000 waste containers. Also at sea, the USSR's fishing industry killed some 45,000 humpback whales between 1946 and 1986. This desperate slaughter stemmed from the issuance by the Central Planning Committee of kill targets that had to be met come what may. Whereas the capitalist Japanese made use of 90 per cent of the meat from the whales they slaughtered, the figure was only 30 per cent for the wasteful Soviets.

The list of Soviet environmental atrocities goes on: the Aral Sea was shrunk by 80 per cent, after planners diverted two rivers to irrigate a desert. Tonnes of pesticides, farm chemicals and weapons were simply dumped in landfill or lakes. Heavy metals, untreated waste, and other pollutants were offloaded into the Caspian Sea. And the Soviet military was no stranger to scorching the Earth.

In practice, collective responsibility means zero responsibility. Under totalitarianism, dissenters stay quiet when the state fouls its nest. Under ideological pressure, scientists abandon truth-seeking and advise governments badly, with bad results. And amid the inefficiency and inertia of collectivism – as opposed to the efficiency and inventiveness of capitalism – the technologies and funds for environmental protection are simply not available. Both communism and Nazism are lessons in government coarseness writ large, coarseness writ deeply into the fabric of people's lives and their surroundings. Bad ideas run amok.

13

The philosopher's tone

Nothing has paralysed intelligence more than the search for scapegoats.

– Theodore Zeldin

When I worked as a teacher, I often took it upon myself to explain my decisions to my pupils. It seemed to me that many of the pupils perceived the school to be a place of arbitrary tasks and arbitrary punishments. In my classes, I had great success in improving the children's commitment and general outlook simply by helping them to understand what school was really for. I'd tell them that the rigours of schoolwork would enhance their thinking, their concentration, their decision-making, their creativity, their life chances, their relationships, their sense of humour, and their happiness. And I'd explain what would happen if mis-behaviour was permitted by the teachers. For instance, if someone threw a pen, or swore, or was disrespectful to me, or rude to a fellow pupil, I'd say, "imagine if we all behaved like that, all the time; imagine how fearful and nasty the school would become!". On this prompting, I think the children understood, hazily, what a tragedy of the commons was, and what they had to do to avoid contributing to such a tragedy in school. They saw, in other words, that their self-interest, my interest, and the interest of their peers coincided to a large degree, and that their behaviour should reflect this.

There was only one instance when my explanatory approach failed. There was a small group of 13- or 14-year-old girls who were lacking focus in my class. I was teaching maths at the time, and they were in the bottom set. Many of the pupils in this set were working heroically, and making great strides in maths; I was determined to get the wayward girls onside, so as not to harm the class as a whole. I asked the girls to stay behind for a few minutes at lunchtime, whereupon I talked to them about their insecurities surrounding maths. I did what I usually did – I explained kindly that, in their end, their lack of effort was hurting themselves and the people around them. I could see by their nodding heads and serious eyes that they were listening intently; I had alerted them to a painful truth about themselves and the situation they were in. They left quite sombrely, but seemingly affected by my words, for the better – or so I thought.

Next lesson, there was an uneasy atmosphere from the start. As usual, I asked the class to pay attention to me while I introduced a new topic. The group of girls were whispering, clustered around their ringleader who was playing with her mobile phone. I asked the ringleader to put the phone away, which she did, grumpily, then I proceeded to begin teaching. A few minutes later, I noticed that the ringleader was fiddling with a device again. I insisted that she put her phone away. She replied, "it's not a phone, it's a calculator". "I'm sorry," I replied; "in that case, please put your calculator down and pay attention to me while I'm speaking". A few seconds later, she was again holding the calculator, staring at the screen and tapping away at the buttons, somewhat theatrically. I repeated my request: "put the calculator down please." The girl replied cheekily, "it's a maths lesson, so I'm allowed to use a calculator". "Not while I'm speaking," I explained: "I need you to pay attention to me, otherwise you won't understand how to do the work." "But I *was* paying attention," the girl replied. "Not fully," I said, with some irritation beginning to show in my voice, to which the girl responded, "why are you picking on me?", then violently swept her books and equipment onto the floor. I asked her to leave the room, whereupon she stood up, yelled "it's so unfair", flounced across to the door, and slammed it on her way out.

In due course, I was standing in the corridor with the girl, armed once again with my explanatory approach; I am stubborn if nothing else. "I wasn't holding a calculator," the girl insisted. "I could see that you were," I replied. "You said I was holding a phone, and it wasn't a phone," she shot back. I responded: "Yes, I corrected that judgment immediately, but you continued to look at your calculator." "I wasn't holding anything," she said, somewhat contradicting her previous statement. "Yes you were," I insisted. "Well, I was still listening to you," she said, hinting once more that she knew exactly what she had been doing. "I wanted you to *look* at me, not just listen to me," I said. "I was looking," she replied, again somewhat contradicting her previous statement. "I could see that you weren't looking," I said. "Well, J--- was on his calculator as well!" she offered, somewhat desperately. "So you *were* on your calculator!" I ventured – thinking I had finally made the logical breakthrough. "No I wasn't," she replied. In exasperation, I sent her to another classroom.

Clearly, the girl was practising self-deception, so as to avoid facing up to her responsibility to herself and her peers. She knew the truth – that she wasn't paying attention, and that she was therefore going to waste the lesson and be a disruptive influence on the people around her – and she knew this reflected badly on her, which is precisely why she was so artfully denying that truth to herself and to me. I understood this much. But I was unprepared for what happened next.

Next lesson, I saw that the girl's deteriorated behaviour had spread. Her friends and her – they must have discussed the situation in the meantime – were appallingly disruptive. The only way I can describe their conduct is to say that they were *hateful* towards me, and I don't believe that is too strong a word. As the weeks progressed, the hate intensified and, naturally, the girls were getting no work done. I simply couldn't influence them. Soon, some of the previously well-behaved boys were angrily misbehaving too – no doubt, trying to impress the girls – until, finally, there was a toxic atmosphere almost throughout the whole class. I was forced to clamp down fiercely, but hardly successfully. The progress of the class had become mired in fury and negativity.

The children had scapegoated me. When, right at the start, I offered those girls a chance to face up to the truth about their attitude and their behaviour, I had inadvertently incentivised them to deny the truth to themselves and blame me instead for their failings in maths. On perceiving clearly their own laziness, the girls simultaneously saw the psychological urgency of hiding their culpability from themselves. As the rewards and pressures of scapegoating spread tragically through the class – including the pleasures of the mob, of righteous anger and personal exoneration – my own increasingly coarse efforts to seize back control only gave the children more reason to scapegoat me. And even when, on numerous occasions, I reverted back to my tried-and-trusted explanatory approach, I was met with irrationality and hostility from almost all the children.

Of course, you might argue, these children may have had problems at home, and you might be right. But that's no explanation for, and certainly no vindication of, their behaviour. I encountered plenty of children in school who had a dreadful domestic life but who had found sanctuary in learning. You might also argue that the children in my class were taught to behave tragically, to avoid responsibility, by our "callous and immoral capitalist society". But that's simply implausible. Even granting the false assumption that capitalism is callous and immoral, I've seen *toddlers* engaging in scapegoating, and they cannot have experienced much of capitalism. I once intervened when two of my nieces – three and four years old – were bickering. After establishing the peace, I returned ten minutes later, by which time they had spontaneously found a powerful way to consolidate their newfound bond, and to propitiate me: they had turned their ire onto my nephew, who was ten months old. "He threw his dinner on the floor", "he broke the spaceship we made out of bricks", "he has stolen our toy". Scapegoating comes naturally to human beings.

And yet it doesn't come at all times, and, when it does come, it doesn't endure indefinitely. Human nature rarely forces us, but rather tempts us, into our behaviour. I only taught maths for a term (I was helping out due to a staff absence) and later that year I bumped into the ringleader who had misbehaved so malignantly in my class. To my amazement, she was smiley and friendly, and apologetic. "I was a nightmare in your class, Sir," she grinned. Trying hard not to be pompous, I said, "that's alright; I'm glad you can see it now; are you getting on a little better in school?". "Yes, I am, Sir, thank you." On other occasions, I bumped into her friends, and they too were pleasant, and acknowledged they had given me a hard time. Somehow these girls had seen the error of their ways.

I don't know how exactly. But an obvious possible factor was the change of teacher. A new context and a new approach could have awakened a new awareness in my former pupils. Another factor was probably the general climate of discipline that prevailed in the school. I was lucky to teach at one of Michael Gove's new 'Academy' schools, and our senior management team set the tone admirably, by placing a relentless emphasis on the children's 'mindset'. Every child was unfailingly encouraged to behave responsibly, and all the teachers unfailingly supported each other when any child failed to live up to expectations.

As well as being subjected to this diffuse but powerful social pressure, my repentant ex-pupils had probably themselves made an effort to improve their attitude and conduct. For most of us, after all, growing up is a process whereby we willingly accept more and more responsibility for our lives. Perhaps, in this light, the self-deception involved in scapegoating is a positive force, at least potentially; you must know the truth in order to lie to yourself about it; maybe sooner or later the truth must prevail over self-deception, like a lifeboat bobbing up to the surface of the sea.

Although my ex-pupils in the end became consciously aware that they had behaved badly, I doubt they ever saw their behaviour specifically as scapegoating. It is possible for a person to realise that he has unfairly blamed someone else in a particular instance, or even to realise this in a series of instances, but still not realise that his behaviour falls into a pattern, that is, into an abstract category. Nor do I think my fellow teachers were explicitly aware of the concept of scapegoating. They tended to emphasise the positive, that is, to emphasise responsibility as opposed to – its opposite – the self-deceptive projection of responsibility onto another. Yet I wonder whether, if my colleagues had explicitly discouraged scapegoating, they could have guided the children even more effectively towards responsibility.

Since working on this book, there have been occasions in my own life when my growing awareness of the concept of scapegoating has influenced my behaviour for the better. On one such occasion, I was working in my part-time job as a delivery boy. I had delivered a curry to a man who was talking on his mobile phone at the time; his distractedness irritated me. For some reason, I inserted the £30 payment he gave me into a pouch pocket on my jumper rather than safely in my wallet. Later – too late – I realised that the money had fallen out in the street while I was cycling along. Rather than accept that I had been careless, I became even more furious with the man for talking on his phone; I felt that he was somehow to blame for my error. I told my colleagues what an idiot the man was. And then... I suddenly realised what I was doing;

I was scapegoating him, of course! The abstract concept of scapegoating penetrated my thoughts like a key in a lock, and released me from my unreasonable brooding. My (not unpleasurable) righteous anger was replaced by embarrassment, and soon my embarrassment was replaced by a sense of calm.

Whether we reach responsibility by way of a positive influence, or by way of a sudden negative realisation that we are unfairly blaming someone else for our own failings, the mindset of responsibility precludes scapegoating. In responsibility, we are simultaneously self-aware and externally aware; we are self-aware insofar as we perceive our own minds, our capacity to choose, and our obligations; and we are externally aware insofar as we understand the situation we are in, and the potential consequences of our choices. Accordingly, responsibility vanquishes scapegoating by preventing us from kidding ourselves about what we know to be true. In the case of the girls in my maths class, if they had acted responsibly they wouldn't have been able to deceive themselves about their laziness, or about the phoney exoneration they were deriving from scapegoating me; nor would they have been able to overlook the tragic effect their behaviour was having on the whole class, not to mention on me, their scapegoated teacher.

In schools, responsibility is (or should be) fostered by teachers. But outside of school, where will such encouragement come from? Who will champion the societal benefits of responsibility? Who will encourage us to contribute to our communities, to charities, to the wider economy? Who will awaken us to the tragic harms of modern scapegoating, of anti-capitalism? Who will beseech us, when it comes to education, health, welfare, housing and the environment, not to irresponsibly delegate our responsibilities to anti-capitalist bureaucrats? We are unlikely to receive much guidance in this matter from the state, nor should we expect it; our deference to condescending, incompetent governance is precisely the problem. Nor, for the time being, are we likely to receive the required guidance from schoolteachers, most of whom are employed by the state and therefore tend to support collectivism outside the classroom. The guidance will have to come from another source.

As a philosopher, I wrote this book because I believe that philosophers ought to accept a large share of the burden for cultivating an atmosphere of responsibility within society. After all, the role of the philosopher is perfectly adapted to this burden. Roughly speaking, there are two aspects to the role. Firstly, philosophers are supposed to reflect on 'the human condition', that is, on the fact that human beings, exclusively among earthly creatures, have an embodied conscious existence, an existence comprised of inner awareness as well as outer awareness. Secondly, based on such reflection, philosophers are supposed to advise other human beings on how to live a good life, on how to adopt a 'worldview' or mindset that leads to living well. Both aspects of the role should lead straightforwardly to responsibility. In reflecting on inner and outer awareness, philosophers ought themselves to become paragons of responsibility. In turn, in giving advice on how to live a better life, philosophers ought to encourage others to become responsible; what else, after all, would constitute responsible advice on how to live well?

By way of their didactic role, philosophers already

enjoy a large influence on society. Other intellectuals – especially in the humanities – tend to hold philosophers in high esteem, and, in turn, intellectuals tend to exert a powerful influence on the attitudes and ideas of university students, who, upon graduating, tend to move into influential jobs, for instance in government and the media. So philosophers have all the more obligation to act with – and set a tone of – responsibility.

Alas, what philosophers ought to do and what they actually do are different things. On the whole, philosophy is – and always has been – a vehicle not for promoting responsibility but for undermining it, inside and outside of philosophy. Yes, philosophers talk fluently – indeed, *ad infinitum* – about inner awareness and outer awareness, about the mind and the world, about the self and the universe, about subjectivity and objectivity, about ideality and reality, about freedom and determinism. But, typically, the purpose of such discourse is not to embrace the human condition and therefore to embrace responsibility, but rather to make a problem out of the human condition so as to eschew responsibility.

Most philosophers insist that the combination of inner awareness and outer awareness comprises a great puzzle. The (inwardly perceived) human mind and the (outwardly perceived) world, so it goes, are so different from each other that their combination doesn't make sense. On the one hand, the human mind is free, self-aware, prone to uncertainty, and uniquely private – only *you* are in your mind, only *I* am in mine. On the other hand, the world comprises a vast agglomeration of objects that lack freedom, self-awareness, doubt, and inner privacy. It seems inexplicable therefore that a mind could arise in such an impersonal world.

Technically speaking, the mind and the world form a 'paradox' – a unity of opposites. By way of an example of a paradox, consider the statement 'I am a liar'. Is the statement true or false? Well, if it is true then it is false, and if it is false then it is true (think about it!); the statement unifies the opposites of truth and falsity. Likewise, the human mind and the world are opposites unified. Via the human brain, the human mind exists in a world that is the very opposite of the mind. On the surface, this mind-world paradox seems to be intolerable, a genuine problem.

Accordingly, philosophers spend most of their time concocting theories that supposedly make the mind-world paradox go away. These theories have one thing in common: they assume that, contrary to appearances, the mind and the world, inner and outer awareness, *do not* exist in combination. There are philosophers who argue that we only ever have knowledge of our own minds; external objects are a fiction created by our minds. There are philosophers who argue the opposite, that our own minds are illusions; we are really just clever robots, complicated objects. There are philosophers who argue that the mind and the world both exist, but not in combination; each exists in a separate realm somehow. There are philosophers (especially among theologians) who argue that there is a 'third thing' – God, or a mystical realm – that supposedly reconciles the mind and the world. And there are philosophers who argue that neither the mind nor the world exists; instead, there is... nothing.

If all this sounds rather pointless to you, you'd be right. After studying philosophy for a decade, and discovering that philosophers have been obsessed with the mind-world problem for thousands of years, I wearily came to a jarring conclusion: the mind and the world seem to form a paradox because they *do* form a paradox. The mind and the world simply *are* opposites unified. Such is the paradox of being human. In other words, to worry about the mind-world paradox is to worry about nothing, to make a normal situation into a 'problem'.

Philosophers who pointlessly make a problem out of the human condition could be described as 'metachondriacs', on an analogy with hypochondria (meta means 'awareness of awareness', so metachondria means 'making a problem out of (inner) awareness of (outer) awareness'). The hypochondriac spuriously assumes that his normal bodily sensations constitute a medical problem, while the metachondriac spuriously assumes that the normal, paradoxical combination of the human mind and the world constitutes a philosophical problem. In so doing, the metachondriac fails to cultivate responsibility – in himself or others. After all, responsibility comprises a combination of inner and outer awareness, whereas the metachondriac deliberately diverts his attention, and that of other people, towards the denial of that combination, the denial of its possibility.

In metachondria, as in hypochondria, the impetus for turning away from responsibility is fear – fear of uncertainty, fear of reality, fear of one's obligations, fear of standing alongside one's fellow men in dealing with reality. Yet, in all of this, the metachondriac, like the hypochondriac, does not consider himself a moral failure. Just as the hypochondriac believes that his spurious medical problem affords him an excuse for inaction, the metachondriac believes that he is preoccupied by a problem that exonerates him from taking responsibility. Similarly, just as the hypochondriac believes that no medical doctor is adequately equipped to alleviate his intractable symptoms, the metachondriac believes that no scientific or practical considerations can be brought to bear on the mind-world problem.

Indeed, the metachondriac considers himself quite the opposite of a moral failure. Just as the hypochondriac believes that his illness elevates him above the fray, such that his pronouncements contain special insight, the metachondriac believes, perversely, that his lack of responsibility makes him a paragon of wisdom; he believes in a sort of phoney perfectionism, where having never tried is supposedly better than having ever failed. More perversely still, other people believe him. By bandying around enlightened-sounding statements about inner and outer awareness, but only ever in the context of abstruse theories that defy common sense, the metachondriac succeeds in bamboozling, and therefore impressing, the public.

In turn, just as the hypochondriac doggedly insists that he really is ill, so as to uphold his excuse for inaction and his alleged moral superiority, the metachondriac vehemently defends the validity of the mind-world problem, so as to uphold his excuse for inaction, and his status. In this light, the various theories that the metachondriac offers as 'solutions' to the mind-world problem say more about his desire to perpetuate the problem than to solve it. His theories are comparable to the spurious 'treatments' by which the hypochondriac supposedly aims to alleviate or cure his symptoms. Neither the hypochondriac's treatments nor the metachondriac's solutions can ever succeed; you can't fix a problem that isn't a problem. The treatments and solutions are, rather, a *manifestation* of a false belief that there is a problem. They are entered into not just for the sake of the hypochondriac or the metachondriac, but for the sake of an audience. What better way to uphold the validity of a problem than to relentlessly try to make it go away?

In attempting to eschew responsibility while simultaneously seizing the moral high ground, metachondriacs are perennially attracted to the notion of 'collective responsibility'. By righteously declaring what 'we' should do, metachondriacs are able to present themselves as paragons of public-spiritedness even as they pass the buck. They don't even pass the buck to anyone in particular, rather to a sort of hive mind that no one controls. The invocation of collective responsibility is cheap – and cheapened – wisdom.

This collective buck-passing reaches its apotheosis in the theory of postmodernism. Metachondriacs who are postmodernists argue that the best way to avoid the mind-world combination is to assert that neither the mind nor the world exists; there are no individual minds, and there is no world. Instead, there is a sort of 'social ether' comprised of a collection of human beings and various forms of human communication, such as speech, writing, symbols, signs, images, gestures, and so on. Inside this all-pervasive social ether, so it goes, we believe that we are individuals with individual minds, and we believe that the world exists, but only because that's what the social ether tells us to believe; the social ether makes it *seem* as though each of us has a mind and lives in a real world. Supposedly, this illusion is the source of all of our problems. If only the social ether – if only *we*, who comprise that ether – would stop presenting ourselves as individuals and stop believing in reality, we could all live happily ever after. Together, we could achieve anything.

Obviously, this theory is bananas, yet postmod ernists – for instance, Michel Foucault, Jacques Derrida, and Richard Rorty – are among the most revered of recent philosophers. Postmodernism affords its proponents an opportunity to vividly display their supposed moral virtue even while utterly rejecting the human condition, and delegating all responsibility, always. Tellingly, the only other philosophical theory that denies the existence of individual minds *and* the real world is nihilism. The social ether has much in common – perhaps everything in common – with nothingness.

Yet the void attracts people. Postmodernism is a drain hole for humanities subjects outside of philosophy itself. Many literary critics, anthropol-ogists, historians and sociologists share the working assumption that the proper object of inquiry for a scholar of the humanities is a social ether whose machinations can be documented without positing individual people or the real world. Postmodernists in these fields do not emphasise the mind-world problem, as the philosopher does, but rather they emphasise the social ether as the target of all sensible inquiry. It is as though these scholars have such a severe case of metachondria that, to them, the mind-world combin-ation is not only a fiction to be overcome through suitable inquiry, but a taboo that shouldn't even be mentioned. Meanwhile, they enjoy all the advantages of metachondria: an excuse for irresponsibility, a socially impressive eschewal of common sense, and an elevated status.

In believing that the mind-world problem exonerates them from responsibility, and in believing that the problem cannot possibly be solved by practical or scientific means, metachondriacs display a chronic indifference to that which they fear (i.e. reality), an indifference exacerbated by their theories. For some metachondriacs – those, for instance, who believe that only the mind exists, or that only a social ether exists, or that the perceived world is a veil of illusion behind which God awaits us – reality drops out of consideration altogether. For other metachondriacs, the mind is separate from reality and therefore ought to be studied *sui generis*. Even those metachondriacs who claim that *only* the world exists – so-called materialists – are somewhat otherworldly. In focusing solely on making a philosophical claim about the world – on winning a theoretical argument against other metachondriacs – materialists ironically fail to pay much attention to the world itself.

Accordingly, one the most bizarre consequences of metachondria is that it tends to divert humanities scholars away from studying human nature, by which I mean the propensities, aspirations and limitations of biological human beings. Learning about human nature can be a great way of enhancing responsibility; by reflecting on the forces that tempt us to behave in one way or another, we can learn how best to marginalise, amplify or channel those forces, in ourselves and others. Moreover, through developing an abstract understanding of those forces, we can learn to resist them directly where necessary; in other words, we can develop self-control, by converting our 'hot' impulses into a 'cold' – calculated – understanding of those impulses. Alas, the theories espoused by meta-chondriacs blot out human nature. If the human mind is the only thing that exists, human nature – as in a biological influence on human behaviour – cannot exist. If God is the origin of the mind and the world, our nature comes from God not from biology. If our mind occupies a separate realm from the world, then our biological nature cannot affect our minds, and so is irrelevant. If the social ether exists then 'we' don't have a biological nature; we make our nature up as we go along. Human nature even gets blotted out by those metachondriacs who are 'materialists', for whom bio-logical human beings are just one aspect of a world that holds no interest beyond its role in a philosophical theory.

Metachondria is a tragedy of the commons. Indeed, it is *the* tragedy of the commons, the tragedy that fuels the tragedy of anti-capitalism and therefore exacerbates all the other tragedies within modern society. The tragic logic of metachondria originates in the rewards that are on offer to philosophers who succumb to the condition. Through metachondria, the philosopher can seem to be fulfilling his self-declared role without going to any of the effort required to fulfil that role. Through talking endlessly about the 'problem' of inner and outer awareness he can seem to be talking about the human condition, while not actually paying any attention to that condition. Through bandying around pointless theories that aim to dismantle responsibility, and through bandying around the notion of collective responsibility, he can seem to be talking about responsibility while simultaneously rejecting responsibility both theoretically, and, as a result, practically. And through the bamboozlement thus created by his theories, he can enhance the kudos that comes with the role of philosopher. In other words, he can seem to fulfil his role in spades even without having to go to any of the trouble of cultivating inner and outer awareness, of embracing freedom and its obligations, of learning about reality and human nature, of acting with responsibility, and of challenging other people to act responsibly. The metachondriac succeeds in making hay as a philosopher without making any hay.

In all of this, metachondriacs are further fortified by the conspiratorial aspect of their condition. By debating each other's pointless theories, in a pseudo-scientific spectacle of constructive disagreement, metachondriacs ordain each other into an intellectual elite within which the rewards of groupishness are amplified by mutually assured esotericism.

As in most tragedies, metachondria is also fortified by self-deception. The metachondriac knows, deep down, that the mind exists in combination with the world. He knows that each opposes the other, and he knows that a paradox is the only means by which such opposites can be unified. He knows, that is, that the mind-world 'problem' doesn't merely stem from what *seems* to be the case, but from what obviously *is* the case, therefore rendering the problem no problem at all. The metachondriac knows, indeed, that the only problem in these matters is his failure to face up to responsibility, and he knows precisely what this problem is worth to him, in terms of his privileges. That's why he so obsessively defends the validity of the mind-world problem, and hides so tenaciously behind pointless theories. Many a time I have asked metachondriacs a specific question: what exactly is *wrong* with the mind-world paradox? I've never received a straight answer, but always a volley of blustering jargon, irrelevant philosophical theorising, and slippery reasoning.

This slipperiness is also in evidence among metachondriacs who invoke collective responsibility even though their theories rule out such a notion. Collective responsibility, after all, is radically inconsistent with all other philosophical theories apart from the nonsense of postmodernism. How can someone who believes, for instance, that only the individual mind exists suddenly believe in society? How can someone who believes that only God truly exists suddenly believe that 'we' are paramount in matters of morality? How can someone who believes that only the world exists suddenly believe that 'we' can choose our morality while no other physical object can? And, similarly, how can someone who believes that the individual mind exists in a realm separate from reality suddenly believe that a hive mind exists too? *Where* do 'we' exist within those two realms? There are no rational answers to these questions. In their rhetorical flight towards collective responsibility, metachondriacs display a logical flightiness that is comparable to the defensive irrationality of any self-deceiving person who knows he is wrong.

The self-deceptive tragedy of metachondria leads naturally to scapegoating. Metachondriacs are characterised by their fear of reality, their aversion to responsibility, and their keenness for unearned distinction in matters of morality. It is natural, therefore, that such people – frightened people who fake an interest in human betterment – will seek a scapegoat to divert attention away from their own moral ineptitude. And it is unsurprising that the chosen culprit is capitalism. The metachondriac believes that his superior wisdom derives from his eschewal of responsibility, from his elevated position above the fray. Down below, he tells himself, is the realm of the mere doers: the working men, businessmen and money makers. With their crass, materialistic, worldly mores, *they* are the contemptible ones.

This verdict on capitalism is reinforced by the tendency of metachondriacs – postmodernists or otherwise – to luxuriate in collective responsibility. Anti-capitalism flows from collective responsibility by way of an answer to an obvious query about 'us': if 'we' are always responsible for producing moral outcomes, and if we are the good guys, then why do so many social problems persist? The only possible answer, according to the logic of collective responsibility, is that 'we' contain a corrupting element, a malevolent force that, *ex hypothesis*, is internal to us, yet, also *ex hypothesis*, is external to our moral consensus. In other words, our collective betterment is being undermined by people who are outsiders as well as insiders – by scapegoats. The obvious culprits are capitalists, the rascals who live among us but trade with strangers. Capitalism is the evil rescuer of collective responsibility.

And, of course, like all scapegoaters, meta-chondriacs are attracted by the psychological benefits of scapegoating; i.e. the pleasures of sadism, guiltlessness, solidarity, cleanliness, irresponsibility, rationalising suffering, enjoying a release from rumination, and avoiding being scapegoated. In securing these benefits, metachondriacs are goaded by their intellects. Seeing yourself as one of the anti-capitalist good guys is all the sweeter when you've got clever 'theories' that prove your righteousness.

Metachondria is a miasma of life-denying, vindictive nonsense that swirls around humanities scholars, especially on university campuses, where it has been absorbed by generations of students, to devastating effect. Having spent years at university being schooled in artful irresponsibility, as well as in collective responsibility and the demonisation of capitalism, humanities graduates are perfectly primed for a career in the blob, in the bureaucratic, anti-capitalist government machine. Like hypochondria, metachondria is all about shouting from the sidelines, achieving social status through social disengagement, exercising control through failing to exercise responsibility – in other words, precisely the job description of an anti-capitalist bureaucrat. From within government, metachondriacs perpetuate their work-shyness and phoney perfectionism, and consummate their animus towards capitalism, by way of laws and regulations that sluice off money and resources from the only people who are capable of generating any. Meanwhile, plenty more humanities graduates, perhaps those who are committed to collective responsibility but less determinedly so, find a career in which they are happily subsidised by taxpayers' money – e.g. in areas of law, business, the media or the arts – without being directly employed by the government.

With so many metachondriacs occupying so many influential positions in society it is no wonder that the public today is suffering from an acute lack of sound advice on how to live well. As a bureaucrat might put it: institutional metachondria leads to a responsibility deficit within wider society. Scourges such as gambling, drugs, obesity, crime, excessive drinking, marital breakdown and spiralling personal debt stem largely from failures of individual responsibility. And, to some extent, so too does the public's modern obsession with technologies of 'distraction' – TV, social media, mobile phones, headphones, video games, and so on. Whether through succumbing to old-fashioned temptations or trivially fixating on digital technologies, people seem happiest these days when they are hiding from themselves and from the situation they are in – from responsibility. In so doing, people also hide from self-knowledge, and self-control. Thanks to metachondria, human nature is seldom talked about and reflected on today; consequently, few people understand themselves, so they drift along without taking responsibility for what they do. Incidentally, this includes the metachondriacs. In keeping with my observations, in chapter 10, about anti-capitalists living chaotically and self-indulgently, in my experience metachondriacs live in the same way but are protected from the consequences of their irresponsibility by their low-stress, high-paying jobs in the blob, just as irresponsible members of the public are protected (to a lesser degree) by welfare. Metachondriac students, similarly, are protected from their irresponsibility – though all the educational grants or loans in the world cannot compensate for the fact that today there are rising levels of mental illness on British campuses, largely due to a responsibility deficit, leading to self-destructive behaviour, in universities.

And, of course, metachondria undermines society

not just via cultural diffusion but by the specific depredations of anti-capitalist governance. From their high perches, metachondriacs conduct the ransacking of capitalism, with all the devastating consequences described in this book. In education, welfare, housing and health, bad behaviour is encouraged by perverse incentives, while professionals such as teachers, doctors and builders are hampered by bureaucratic intrusions. In the economy, overzealous regulation suffocates small businesses and cossets big businesses, leading to demoralisation and over-ripe inequality. And under the banner of environmentalism, the government implements worthless or backfiring 'green' policies, while squandering the wealth and efficiency of the markets.

In all of this, our metachondriac masters turn a blind eye to reality, including the reality of human nature. Anyone with any common sense can see that anti-capitalist bureaucratic intrusions into education, welfare, housing, health and the wider economy must founder, and indeed have foundered, on the bedrock of reality and human nature. It is simply not possible to pool the resources of millions or billions of people without causing grotesque levels of inefficiency, corruption, freeloading and poverty. Only by deceiving themselves about this fact can metachondriacs persist with their futile plans. Only by deceiving themselves that they care for the poor can metachondriacs justify their remoteness from, and indifference to, the lives that they have wrecked. Sadly, intellectuals may be the most prolific self-deceivers of all; those who can reason well can also rationalise well. As Thomas Sowell has noted: 'Socialism in general has a record of failure so blatant that only an intellectual could ignore or evade it.' Saddest of all, by turning their backs on inner and outer awareness, and therefore on reality and human nature, metachondriacs leave vast expanses of human possibility unexplored and untapped. Collective responsibility is a comfort blanket thrown over the heads of intellectuals.

Amid government depredations and an atmosphere of frivolous unrealism and diffuse irresponsibility – in other words, amid socialism – people become less sociable. Influenced by metachondriacs, they make excuses for not participating, for failing to add to the stock of social capital. Clubs, committees, societies and teams wither; even in child rearing, people fail to see the value of community spiritedness. Getting together to improve the local area seems pointless when the government is supposedly getting the whole nation, nay the whole world, together. Many times I have heard people completely – determinedly – miss the point about social capital; they ask, "what is our nasty Tory government going to do to promote communities?". It is *not* the government's job to make us get off the sofa and participate in a community. (I'm reminded of the old adage that says 'you're not stuck in traffic; you *are* traffic'. A lack of communal life is not a tragedy imposed upon you; if you're sitting at home on the sofa, you *are* a lack of community.) Nor is it the government's job to act charitably on our behalf. In granting the state this role, we become less charitable.

Under the influence of metachondria, people also shun that vast theatre of cooperation otherwise known as the 'commercial sector'. Getting one's hands dirty by trading with greedy capitalists seems unnecessary when the government, supposedly, is perfectly capable of spreading wealth.

In turn, the influence of metachondria even compromises people who *are* open to trade, by inclining them to shun the wide openness of social capitalism. Wide openness means trading while refusing to profit from inflicting upon other communities harms that one wouldn't inflict upon one's own community; for instance, a wide open trader might refuse to contribute to tragedies such as manipulative marketing, implanting sugar in food, scaremongering in the media, glamourising gambling, encouraging unnecessary litigation, and damaging the environment. These tragedies of coarseness, and others like them, are endemic in capitalism but are kept in check by social capital, insofar as communities both protect their own members against the coarse behaviour of outsiders and encourage insiders to adopt an attitude of wide openness. Shorn of social capital, and also shorn of resources thanks to punitive taxes and regulations, capitalism becomes a breeding ground for tragedies of coarseness. Businesses become less likely to treat and pay their staff well, train an apprentice, employ someone out of decency or loyalty, strive for quality not superficial appeal, charge an honest price, provide a friendly 'human' service to customers, or patronise local arts.

Under the pressure of relentless scapegoating, individuals likewise become coarser, hoarding their wealth and evading or avoiding their taxes. In all its forms, the coarseness of scapegoated capitalism further motivates – and consolidates – the preeminence of government metachondriacs. In their eyes, capitalism's coarseness is both unwelcome and welcome. The more capitalism displays unwelcome qualities, the more its assets and privileges supposedly deserve to be confiscated, a practice perfectly welcome to meta-chondriacs, who, after all, cannot live off irresponsibility alone. The more capitalism is forced to make amends, the more metachondria thrives.

The spoils of scapegoated capitalism ultimately make their way back to the source of metachondria – to universities. In Britain, only five higher education institutions are not financed by the government. And, individually, the vast majority of academics are, at least to some extent, dependent on government funding. To acquire this funding involves navigating a bureaucratic assault course of astonishing complexity and absurdity. Just as businesses are forced to waste their time gathering hopefully around the carcass of state money, academics waste much of their careers filling out countless funding application forms, whereby arrogant bureaucrats assess the alleged 'social impact' of each research proposal.

This expensive process is another aspect of the tragedy of metachondria – a sort of echo of meta-chondria. Typically, the bureaucrats who manage the funds are steeped in metachondria, having originally qualified for their government jobs by completing a humanities degree. The apprentices thereby become the masters: academics must demonstrate the strength of their metachondria to their erstwhile students. This perverse imperative has intensified the tragedy of metachondria. Humanities scholars have always competed with each other to see who can display the most bamboozling and impressive irresponsibility, in the form of the most artfully vituperative protestations against personal responsibility and capitalism, and the most articulate elegies to collective responsibility. But now these scholars must compete predominantly for the endorsement of fellow ideologues (including their colleagues, from whom references are required by the bureaucrats), as opposed to competing for the attention of a potentially sceptical public. As a result, meta-chondria is being refined and consolidated as never before. The air is thick with it on campuses, to the extent that free speech is under threat in the very places where it should be protected the most, as commentators such as Steven Pinker and Jonathan Haidt have noted. Universities today are deeply forbidding places for anyone who believes in common sense, human nature, and responsibility.

Amid such a frenzy of denunciation, fuelled by postmodernists above all, scientists, too, are increas-ingly pandering to the metachondriacs and leaping aboard the anti-capitalist bandwagon. When the major-ity of intellectuals are basking in the ersatz wisdom of collective responsibility, only a sucker would go to the effort of cultivating genuine wisdom, through cultivat-ing genuine responsibility, in oneself and others. This tragic logic makes an especially strong impression among scientists who study inanimate matter and therefore know little about human nature yet who also wish to display their intellectual superiority in matters of morality. Geologists, physicists, biologists, physiol-ogists, chemists, engineers – when pontificating on what human beings ought to do, these physical scientists are perennially attracted by the prospect of luxuriating in the phoney public-spiritedness of collective responsibility.

Another attraction of collective responsibility to some scientists is that it affords them the opportunity to engage in moral showmanship without jeopardising their dismal belief that all human behaviour, just like any physical system, must be determined by causal laws: human behaviour, so it goes, is entirely caused by the social environment we live in, so 'we' ought to create a better society, oughtn't we?

Even scientists who have a good understanding of human nature sometimes pander to metachondria, thus squandering the potential utility, in themselves and others, of science-based self-knowledge. It is easier – less confrontational, and less philosophically controversial – for scientists to argue that the more we learn about ourselves the more we understand how power*less* we are as individuals. Some scientists go as far as to say that our behaviour is entirely determined by human nature, or by human nature combined with our social milieu; in neither case do we as individuals have a choice as to how we behave; our minds are simply vehicles. Once again, when these scientists are pressed on moral matters, collective responsibility is a constant temptation. Accustomed to talking about human beings as a species, it is a short step for scientists, whenever they are required to say something wise and positive-sounding, to talk about what 'we' should do as a species. The freedom artificially denied to our individual nature becomes a power artificially granted to a collective 'us'.

Indeed, amid an academic environment so hostile to human freedom and responsibility, no wonder some environmental scientists have, as we have seen, entirely subjugated the values of free enquiry and critical realism to the nonsense of postmodernism. No wonder normal science is, in this way, being sidelined by a desperate animosity towards reality, and towards capitalist scapegoats, such that scientific truth about the environment has become hard to distinguish from a banner for a government agenda.

Where will it end? Must it end in the social, economic and environmental devastation of scapegoatalitarianism? Must we doggedly insist on collective responsibility, as they did in Nazi Germany and communist Russia, even as our civilization crumbles around us? Must our metachondriac masters squeeze scapegoated capitalism until it bleeds to death? Or will the scapegoating of capitalism somehow reach *its* end? The prospect of a cessation originating from within the government is slim. Nobody gives up power readily. Perhaps, instead, the change will come from within the populace, through the public's democratic de-selection of the scapegoaters; but, arguably, the constituency of capitalism is already so small, and the constituency of anti-capitalism so big, that the requisite democratic influence is unavailable. And there is also the problem of anti-capitalism's long march through the institutions; the electorate, and elected governments, seem to be powerless to halt that march, even if they wanted to.

No, I think anti-capitalism must end – or perhaps I should say the end of anti-capitalism must begin – in the realm of ideas, especially with philosophers, and, in turn, with humanities scholars influenced by philosophy. Metachondria's carping, goading influence that blasts out from the bullhorn of academia must quieten down before anti-capitalism will release its frenzied grip on society. Granted, within academia, as within governance, metachondria is a tragedy of the commons, to which intellectuals succumb by way of the individual advantages of eschewing responsibility and professing ersatz wisdom. Therefore, only by renouncing those advantages can metachondriacs begin to foster the atmosphere of responsibility that modern society so desperately needs. But it is reasonable to hope that, within academia, meta-chondriacs might prove more malleable than they are elsewhere. Academics, despite the pressure latterly placed upon them by the government, are freer than most of us to explore, reject or embrace ideas – in other words, to shape their lives according to an internal voice of conscience.

Whatever their position within – or perhaps I should say, astride – society, metachondriacs must look inwards and outwards, and look hard. Inwards to their freedom, their obligations, their crass desire for cheap wisdom, and their fear of reality. And outwards to reality itself, which, along with the reality of human nature, poses an eternal challenge to freedom, a challenge that evidently can never be met adequately by collective responsibility. Ultimately, metachon-driacs must face up to their existence, paradoxical as that existence is, with its human face pressed up against the cold reality of an impersonal universe. These truths are a lifeboat submerged in the self-deception of metachondria. Let's hope that the lifeboat bobs up soon, that the metachondriacs might row it away from the luxury liner of irresponsibility and towards the shores of good sense. There, intellectuals might start over, responsibly – by embracing, not denigrating, community-spiritedness and economic openness, especially wide openness. And, above all, by contributing to the long and arduous task of campaigning against anti-capitalist governance, against the so-called 'socialism' that has inflicted so much harm – and threatens to inflict more – upon capitalists, upon businesses, upon the poor, upon children, upon the sick, upon the environment, upon us all.

If philosophers ought to be vigilant towards self-deception, to look inwards unflinchingly, then perhaps I should conclude by doing the same. It wouldn't be the first time: I used to be a socialist. Everything I've said here about the mindset of the anti-capitalist, I've discovered by reflecting on my own failings. Today, I believe that the picture I have painted in this book is broadly accurate, but I admit of course that the reality of politics and governance is always more complex than anyone can convey. I admit that not all people who work for the government are anti-capitalists. I admit that not all anti-capitalists favour centralised government. I admit that not all philosophers are metachondriacs, humanities scholars even less so, and I admit that not all metachondriacs suffer from the condition all of the time. I admit that not all anti-capitalists are metachondriacs, and not all metachondriacs are anti-capitalists. I admit that not everything every anti-capitalist or metachondriac says or does, whether in government or otherwise, is unhelpful. I even admit that democracy can benefit from a political force that emphasises the common good – if only socialists would provide that emphasis, rather than contributing to backfiring anti-capitalist governance.

I admit, moreover, that it would be utterly wrong to encourage a tit-for-tat witch-hunt against anti-capitalists. No one wants to see a return to the days of McCarthyism. Capitalism's call for freedom must be just that, no less and no more. Anti-capitalism and metachondria must be tolerated in the name of the very freedom and responsibility that they define themselves in opposition to.

And I admit that I, too, might yet be a scapegoater, so deep is the tendency within human nature towards scapegoating. It hasn't escaped my notice that I am *blaming* anti-capitalists for their failings. For all I have been able to discover through my inner and outer awareness, through my quest to philosophise more responsibly, I too could be deceiving myself; I could be self-deceptively projecting blame onto others. Perhaps there is a form of meta-scapegoating, wherein a scapegoater accuses his scapegoat of scapegoating. Am I so artfully devious? I don't believe it. If the anti-capitalists do, then they ought to take my arguments apart, point by point, rationally, self-consciously and realistically. That, as I see it, would be progress in itself.

29943250R00144

Printed in Great Britain
by Amazon